The Rede Va

He'll sing Redewater's muir
  Where whirring heath-co.
Where limpid wells and heather bells
  Delight the sportsman's e'e.

Robert Roxby, 1809

For the modern traveller intent on making the journey to or from Scotland, the traditional route to follow is the A68 trunk road which runs through the valley of the River Rede. It is a picturesque highway which can be hazardous in winter when drifting snow blocks the twisting Border pass. Many of these travellers have no desire to stop, particularly those going north, for they are drawn by the urge to reach Carter Bar, where the road crosses the frontier between England and Scotland at a point marked by a massive monolith.

But for the traveller who does have the time and the inclination to linger, the valley of the Rede, 'a verie prettie water', has much to offer. It is a valley of contrasts where ancient woodlands are dwarfed by huge blocks of modern forest; where the brown expanse of moors is enriched by the small secret burns that tumble through on their way to the Rede. The valley is a treasure house for the naturalist and provides rare delights for the walker and rider.

Redesdale's greatest treasure is its history, for this is the valley which is richer in story and ballad than any other in England. Prehistoric man built his settlements here, the Romans established themselves at High Rochester and buried their dead in a cemetery nearby. The most bitter battle in the medieval Anglo-Scottish wars was fought at Otterburn, the Border Reivers carried on their 'deadlie feuds' from their strongholds in the valley. The 17th century Covenanters held their secret meetings in the hills, whisky smugglers and drovers used the old Roman road of Dere Street, and the murderer William Winter met his end on the gibbet above Elsdon. The violence and stubborn courage, bloodshed and romance, triumphs and tragedies continue to excite the imagination of present-day historians, novelists and poets in much the same way as they stimulated the pens of William Camden, Sir Philip Sidney and Walter Scott long ago.

1

The inhabitants of Redesdale had achieved infamy as early as 1413. In that year an eminent Catholic priest, Aenaeas Sylvius, later Pope Pius II, journeyed through the area and noted that the men were small, bold and easily roused and their women fair, comely and pleasing, but not distinguished by their chastity. In 1421 the Westminster Parliament was deluged with complaints against the thieves and felons who lived in the valley and in 1498 Fox, Bishop of Durham, was forced to threaten them all with the terrors of excommunication. By the 16th century it was universally recognised that the people of Redesdale were savages and rank robbers who were, to use Camden's words 'stubborn and uncivil'. So notorious were they that the incorporated Society of Merchant Adventurers of Newcastle passed a bye-law in 1564 forbidding any of their members to apprentice a Redesdale or Tynedale man because 'the parties there brought up are known either by education or nature, not to be of honest conversation; and they commit frequent thefts and other felonys'.

They were a quarrelsome lot: witness the dispute between Percival Reed, Laird of Troughend, and Isaac Marrowe, Rector of Elsdon. When the Rector refused to waive a penance, Reed pulled his beard and called him 'a base priest and stinking caistrel'. Reed was summoned before the Bishop for this, fined £10 and ordered to acknowledge his offence publicly in Elsdon church. It was his wife, however, who on the appointed day performed that penance, stating that her husband was sick and could not attend.

By the 18th century the more violent characteristics of earlier times were redirected into bouts of gambling, drinking and cock-fighting, which plunged many into debt and forced them to sell their lands and tenancies. William Howard, who had held the manor of Redesdale, died in a debtors' prison in Marshalsea in 1777, while Gabriel Hall's debts compelled him to sell his property at Monkridge Hall in 1783 to Robert Lisle, a Morpeth attorney. Overindulgence in alcohol in the 19th century contributed to the decay and eventual sale of many properties which had been held by the same family for generations. In 1918, the then Lord Redesdale's gambling debts to King Edward VII necessitated the sale of nine farms in the valley.

Redesdale is still a rich source of scandalous and amusing tales, and tradition has it that 'Redewatter bred, Redewatter aye till dead'.

Early Man

They inhabit wild and waterless mountains and desolate and marshy plains, having no walls nor cities nor tilled land, but living off flocks and wild animals and some fruits. They live in tents, naked and unshod, holding their women in common and rearing their offspring together. Such is the island of Brettania and such its inhabitants, at least of the hostile part of it.

Cassius Dio, c. A.D. 200

Man's first presence in Redesdale was about 6,000 years ago. Some of the most interesting remains of early settlement are the monuments raised to honour the dead. One example is the long cairn on Bellshiel Law excavated in 1935. It is approximately 112m long and although no burial was found, similar structures examined elsewhere in Britain show that several burials were normally deposited in one cairn over a period of years. Archaeological investigation of long cairns suggests that they were confined to the period 3500–2000 BC.

Another long cairn lies on Dour Hill. Nearby is a burial ground used by a later Bronze Age community. At this time, between about 2000 and 650 BC, it was common practice to place the dead lying on their side in a crouched position in a stone-lined cist, which was sealed by a large slab and then covered by a round cairn. In 1976, foresters disturbed one of these burials and a rescue excavation was undertaken. Teeth and the fragmented skulls of an eleven year old child and an infant of 6–9 months were found in the cist. A food vessel resting on its side on the floor of the cist contained hazel-nut shells. A large area of burning on the old land surface near the grave showed where ceremonial rites had been performed. This burial probably took place between about 1900–1500 BC; similar food vessels found elsewhere have been securely dated to that period.

3

Cup and Ring rock carving

Another large Bronze Age cairn on the haugh between Otterburn village and the River Rede was dismantled in 1729 when 60 tons of stone were carted away. The cist apparently contained charcoal and burnt bones. Other notable cairns exist in the area but all of them have been disturbed in the past by grave robbers who understandably left no record of any finds.

The earliest habitation site yet found in Redesdale is on Tod Law where there are the remains of three round timber huts dating to the Bronze Age. Another Bronze Age settlement in the valley, the subject of a recent excavation, is known to have been occupied between 1000–700 BC.

Three larger earthworks near Otterburn also testify to the presence of Romano-British settlements which occur on both sides of the Rede at intervals of about a kilometre down the length of the valley, close to the modern farms from which their names are derived. The settlements were linked by trackways such as that along Rooken Edge. 3,000 years later traders still frequented these routes. Tinkers, tailors and grocers hawking their wares, clerics like the indefatigable Thomas Newlands, plodded on horse-back or on foot along these well-worn paths, many of which are now public rights of way.

Ritual too, played an important part in the life of early man, but rock carvings, so numerous elsewhere in Northumberland, are scarce in Redesdale. The only outstanding example is on Tod Crag, Ottercops, with a group of burial cairns nearby.

By following a forest trail – up through the trees on the south side of the Rede – and scrambling on across rough country, it is possible to reach some standing stones on a hillside overlooking Cottonshopeburnfoot. They are romantically called 'The Three Kings'; the inconvenient fourth stone lies partly hidden in the undergrowth. These sandstone blocks, the largest of which weighs 2½ tons, were probably erected in the same period as the Goatstones near Simonburn, and as the better known standing stones and stone circles throughout Britain – some time around 2000 BC. The ceremonies which took place can only be surmised; the stones survive but they are, unfortunately, silent.

Excavation of Iron Age hut at Woolaw

The Romans in Redesdale

A vexillation of the Fourth Cohort of Gauls and a vexillation of the Second Cohort of Nervians set this up.

A building inscription from High Rochester,
found in a garden wall, 1982.

For almost four centuries Britain was ruled by Rome and throughout much of that time the Rede valley played a key role in maintaining military control over the north of the province.

Twenty five years after the Romans under Claudius invaded southern Britain in AD 43, Julius Agricola's troops swept through the whole of the north from Yorkshire to the Firth of Tay in Scotland. Unlike the south, however, the north was never completely pacified. The army did not move on, leaving the native population free of military occupation; instead it stayed – in force – to police the area and to carry out more serious military manoeuvres if necessary. The effectiveness of such a policy was based upon a well-planned network of roads and forts north of the demarcation line of Hadrian's Wall.

Dere Street, the most vital communication link between southern and northern Britain, cuts right across Redesdale. Much of it is still in use today as the A68 and a short distance from the road, on the left, as it breasts the top of the hill going north out of West Woodburn, is a Roman milestone, one of only three which survive in Northumberland. After Blakehope, Dere Street is visible only as a grass-grown track until it climbs up out of the Sills Burn, to become once more a tarmac road for the modern army on the Redesdale Artillery Range.

Roman milestone near Corsenside

Once established, the communication links were maintained by a series of camps. There are fourteen known permanent or temporary camps and two minor forts; they have been placed either to house the men when the road was under construction or repair, or to give overnight shelter for people travelling along the road. It is also possible that these camps were established for regular military training in much the same way as the Otterburn Training Area is used today.

Two large forts, at Risingham *(Habitancum)* and High Rochester *(Bremenium)* gave additional protection. Risingham now shows up merely as grass covered mounds, but in the 3rd century it housed 1,000 cavalry and a unit of mounted scouts, the *'exploratores Habitancenses'.* Of the two forts, High

Rochester, 14km north of Risingham, was the more strategically important because of its commanding position above the Sills Burn, with uninterrupted views to the north and west. The Roman name for the fort was *Bremenium,* which means the Place of the Roaring Stream. When the Sills Burn is in full spate the thundering waters can be clearly heard in High Rochester.

The visible remains which cover an area of about 2ha date to the 3rd and 4th centuries. But the first fort on the site was probably built by Agricola in the early 80s. High Rochester housed a unit of 1,000 cavalry. During its occupation it was garrisoned in turn by units from Spain, France, Belgium and Yugoslavia. In the 3rd century the garrison was augmented by mounted scouts, the *'exploratores Bremenienses'.* In later centuries Bremenium was used as a source of building stone. Some of the more distinctive masonry, such as guttering and ballista balls, have been built into the porch of the former village school, situated at the junction of the A68 and the road leading to the fort. Many squared blocks have been incorporated within local field walls and cottages, especially in the village of High Rochester itself. John Hodgson, writing in 1827, recorded that in 1810 two Presbyterian ministers, Mr Jollie and Mr Hope, removed the south gate and most of the facing stones from the south, east and north walls of the fort. Now all there is to see of the fort's perimeter is part of an interval tower immediately to the west of the south gateway, the bottom courses of one side of the north gate and the magnificent west gate.

Of the interior of the fort which was excavated in the early 1850s no buildings are visible; any remains lie hidden beneath the village green. High Rochester grew up as a village inside the walls of the old Roman fort; the old Pele or bastle house and the three cottages, the middle one of which was also a bastle, are now all that survive of a once thriving community.

The Romans left more than just roads and defences. Less than a kilometre south-east of High Rochester stand the lower courses of a circular stone tomb, which presumably held the cremated remains of an officer of the fort's garrison. On two opposite stones are carved the worn reliefs of a pine cone and the horned head of a deer, symbols associated with death in the Roman world. Other tombs close by were destroyed by excavation in the early 1850s and the stones were used to build a nearby sheep stell. Over fifty graves of the less wealthy members of the garrison lie in circular earth mounds on lower ground in a cemetery close to the deserted farm of Petty Knowes.

The Officer's Tomb, Petty Knowes

7

Most of the portable Roman antiquities from Redesdale are in the Museum of Antiquities in Newcastle or in the Duke of Northumberland's collection in Alnwick Castle, but a few still remain in the valley in Horsley and Elsdon churches and some of the older farms and houses. The best known relic is at Parkhead, near West Woodburn. Sculpted in high relief on the rock face of a disused quarry are the plump legs – all that survive – of the figure called locally 'Rob of Risingham', probably a local god adopted by the garrison at Habitancum. A smaller representation of Rob has been made by Ron Charlton of West Woodburn and was erected alongside the remains of the original relief by the Redesdale Society in 1983.

All that remains of Rob of Risingham

The Ancient Forest of Redesdale

They hunted high, they hunted low,
By heathery hill and birken shaw;
They raised a buck on Rooken Edge
And blew the mort at fair Ealylawe.

Ballad of Parcy Reed

Six thousand years ago the forest of Redesdale consisted of open glades and thickets of deciduous woodland stocked with deer, bears, wolves, wild boar and small game. Family groups of hunters seeking clothing, tools and meat were seasonal visitors arriving in the valley in spring and leaving with the onset of winter. Few traces remain of their presence or of their successors in Roman or later times, but in the 12th century Redesdale became one of the great royal hunting forests of the realm where beasts and birds dwelt in the safe protection of the King 'for his delight and pleasure'.

For almost 400 years after the Norman Conquest, the Lordship of Redesdale was held by the Umfraville family. At some time between 1182 and 1199, on the marriage of his sister Alicia to William Bertram, Robert de Umfraville granted 'the whole of my forest of Altercoppes and of Ellesden, with the game and the land and with all other liberties belonging to the said forest saving only my villages'. Bertram was also to have 'four groundes on the west of Rede called Crossensete, the Snape of Wodeburne, Smoltewelford (Raylees?) and Redesbank and they shall have the hunting with their men and dogs with the horn, bow and arrows, without hindrance from anyone, and at all seasons of the year'. The lands so granted were to be held by their heirs, free from all suits and services, by the payment of one sparrowhawk annually to de Umfraville and his heirs. By 1324, the forest bounds encompassed '20 acres of wood and 200 acres of waste at Nuthope, 100 acres of wood and 200 acres of waste at Cotinghope, 300 acres of wood at Kyneshope and 100 acres of wood in Yardhope'. Three hundred years later, James I's grant of Redesdale to Theophilus, Lord Howard of Walden included 'the chase called Wilkwood Forest or the Forest of Ridleys'.

Since hunting was so important to the King and his barons, special laws were imposed to ensure not only that the forest remained 'the safe mansion of wild beasts' but also to protect the trees which gave them shelter. Those who lived in the forest could graze cattle and pigs there and take dead wood for fuel, but they were forbidden to carry bow and arrows. If they kept a dog it had to be 'lawed' by cutting out its front pads so that it could not chase game. The one exception was mastiffs, which had to lose three claws from each forepaw. Anyone who failed to comply was fined 3 shillings. In 1199, Richard de Umfraville persuaded King John to grant him the privilege that 'none should graze their cattle, hunt or fell wood in his forests of Redesdale and Coquetdale'. Until 1217 when the forest clauses of Magna Carta were issued as a separate Charter of the Forest, poachers were punished by mutilation or even death. After 1217 they could expect imprisonment and heavy fines. An army of officials was appointed to rid the forest of wolves and also enforce the laws of trespass, however since most were local men who probably sympathised with the trespassers, a blind eye was often turned to forest offences.

Whilst the forest laws imposed severe penalties for poaching, it was more difficult to control the clearance of the trees which had begun about 3000 BC. When man started farming he naturally confined his efforts to one locality, and to create cultivation plots for crops and grazing for stock he first cleared the woodland. Using stone and flint axes and mattocks to slash the undergrowth and fell the trees, he then used the timber for stockades, houses and fuel, a practice which was to continue for many centuries. In his *'Itinerary'*, Henry VIII's Antiquary, John Leland, commented on the lack of wood in Northumberland. The royal commissioners, Bowes and Ellerker, in the Border Survey of 1541, laid the blame firmly on the Scots who came to 'steale and carrye awaie much of the said wood which ys to them a great proffyte foe the maynte'unce of their houses and buyldinge'. They were still being blamed for doing it in 1598.

Encroachment on the forest was a gradual, but unremitting process. As pasture farming intensified domestic animals, particularly cattle and sheep, browsed on young seedlings with the result that natural regeneration was impeded. By 1827 John Hodgson recorded that most of the deciduous woodland had disappeared: 'between the hills are broad and flat morasses called flow mosses, many of which have been the sites of ancient woods of willow, birch and alder; in some of them oaks are found and others contain forests of buried pines'.

Although the destruction was temporarily halted by the planting of shelter and amenity belts for sporting purposes by the big landowners in the 19th century, the final inroads were made this century by the two World Wars when Britain was forced to produce her own timber. Today the head of Redesdale is once again afforested, but with dense stands of Norway and Sitka spruce and Japanese larch, forming the modern equivalent of the ancient forests of Northumberland.

The clearance of the old forest also affected the wildlife, which began to decline. A 16th century report by the Warden responsible for the safety of Redesdale against wolves and robbers, states plainly 'there be no wolves'. In

fact the last wolf in England is reputed to have been killed on Wolf Crag, one mile south of Ottercops. But small game has survived and local people still retain some of the hunting, fishing and food gathering traditions of their forbears.

Others prefer to indulge their passion for the chase by following the hounds. The Umfravilles hunted with a mixed pack, one heavily-built hound led on a leash for starting the quarry from its lair, several couples of greyhounds which hunted by sight and a larger number of ordinary hounds which followed the scent. Now the chase is confined to fox-hunting. The present Redesdale pack, the Border, dates back to at least 1857 and it is believed that the hounds, which are all brachettie (i.e. scent followers) are of the same strain which existed in 1874. Until 1951, the Mastership was held by two old-established Redesdale families, the Robsons and the Dodds, but since 1952 the Hedley family of Overacres has provided the Master and John Dixon of Rochester has been Whipper-in. The hunting season officially begins on 1st November to end at lambing time in April. The Border pack follows the scent from south of Bellingham in North Tynedale up through Redesdale, out on to Cheviot and across the Border itself as far as Hownam in Roxburghshire, riding over the same fells as did their reiving ancestors in the troubled times of long ago.

Michael Hedley, MFH with the Border Foxhounds

A Troubled Border

These borders are in most lamentable condition, looking for and expecting justice, yet all is overthrown, as for exsampell in the wryghtinge of this littyl letter, I have byn caled dowen severall tymes to se the freshe bledinge bluddey woundes and hortes that have byn geven this last night bey the Scottes, whoe never ley styll on nighte.

Sir John Carey, 1597

Redesdale is part of England's northern border territory; its character and history have been influenced by the evolution of the Border line. The boundary between England and Scotland is an artificial creation and its wavering line reflects the ebb and flow of centuries of political intrigue and military confrontation.

In the Roman period Hadrian's Wall was the frontier between northern and southern Britain and the decision to site the Wall where it is, was based on topography rather than on any racial or cultural differences. The native British tribal territory thus created between the Wall and the southern uplands of Scotland, was used as a buffer zone against the aggressive Caledonian tribes to the north. When the Angles invaded they moved inland from the east coast and so the old Roman road of Dere Street became the new frontier. The Anglian kingdom of Northumbria to the east of this line, stretched as far north as the Firth of Forth. By the eve of the Norman Conquest the frontier had changed yet again, for the Scots had pushed the English back to an east-west border formed by the Rivers Tweed and Solway. In the face of this threat, English frontier defences had to be improved so Redesdale was given a special status. It was made a 'Liberty', i.e. an area where the King's authority was wielded by his nominee the Lord of Redesdale, who provided the men to defend the border lands.

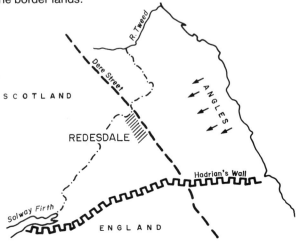

When William the Conqueror arrived in England he was quick to realise the strategic importance of the Liberty. He granted the Lordship of Redesdale to his kinsman Robert de Umfraville, who was excused from military service on condition that he kept the Liberty free from enemies and wolves. The Liberty incorporated most of Upper Redesdale and Upper Coquetdale and in effect was a large petty kingdom under the rule of the Umfravilles.

The most infamous member of the family was Gilbert, first Earl of Angus, who succeeded to the Lordship in 1245. He so frequently exceeded his authority that finally in 1293 he was brought before the Newcastle Assize. Charges against him were *(a)* that he erected a gallows at Alwinton without licence from the crown, *(b)* that his bailiffs fined both those who appeared and those who failed to appear before his courts whether they lived in the Liberty or not, *(c)* that when he seized the cattle of John of Hirlaw for grazing on common land, he sold two of them and had three more killed for his kitchen! In defence Gilbert argued that his office entitled him to many privileges: no sheriff or other bailiff of the King had the right to enter the Liberty of Redesdale to exercise authority; all legal cases concerning the Liberty were to be heard in *his* courts before *his* justices; he could free criminals from his gaol at Harbottle at his own discretion and deal with abuses concerning the inspection of bread and ale. Moreover, he could confiscate the chattels of fugitives and the free-grazing land of felons. He claimed the river-crossing tax at Elishaw (which he said he only exacted from Scotsmen), the right to hold a market at Harbottle every week on Tuesdays and an annual fair on 8th September as well as a Sunday market at Elsdon and an annual fair there on 16th August.

Despite the Lord of Redesdale's intermittent high-handedness the Border lands throughout this time remained fairly peaceful, but by the end of the 13th century, the growing might of Scotland was seen as a serious threat to England's national security. When Alexander III of Scotland fell and broke his neck in 1286, leaving his infant grand-daughter as Scotland's Queen, Edward I of England seized the opportunity to seek control over his rival's kingdom. In the ensuing wars, Redesdale, like many other Border valleys, was ravaged by the opposing armies. It was not until 1328 that England agreed to recognise Scotland's independence, but the conflicts had aroused such fierce national hatred, which had never before existed on the Borders, that despite the peace the warring Border barons were determined to continue the struggle. The most dramatic of these forays inspired what is probably the oldest folk ballad in the country – the 'Battle of Otterburn', which tells of the battle fought between the English under Sir Henry Percy (Shakespeare's Harry Hotspur) and a Scottish raiding party led by James, Earl of Douglas.

The Battle of Otterburn, 1388

In 1580 Sir Philip Sidney wrote 'I never heard the olde song of Percy and Duglas, that I found not my heart moved more than with a Trumpet'. The exact date of this glorified skirmish is not certain. Although the chronicler Sir John Froissart gives it as 19th August, it may have been much earlier in the month, as the first verse of the ballad suggests:

> Yt fell abowght the Lamasse tyde, (Old Lammas day – 1 August)
> When husbondes wynnes ther haye, (farmers cut their hay)
> The dowghtye Douglasse bowynd him to ryde,
> in Yngland to take a praye. (go on a raid.)

In the high summer of 1388, Douglas came over the Border with an army of 4,000 picked men, set fire to 'three good towers on Redeswire fells' and ravaged much of Northumberland and Durham. Later, during a brief struggle outside Newcastle, he captured the pennant of the city's defender, Sir Henry Percy. Douglas taunted Percy to give chase and do battle for the pennant before the raiders reached the safety of Scottish soil. The challenge was accepted, for rivalry between the two men was intense.

They agreed to meet near Otterburn. After Douglas left Newcastle, Percy set off in hot pursuit with a force of 8,000 men, and caught up with his foe. Without giving his army a chance to recover from their forced march, he attacked at dusk even though he knew that 7,000 reinforcements under the Bishop of Durham were on their way. The opposing armies fought beneath the thin light of the moon.

> Ther the fowght the day, and all the nyght,
> And many a dowghtye man was slone.

The Battle Seat near Bennettsfield

Sir George Trevelyan referred to it as a 'midnight battle of heroes ending in an English rout'. Douglas was killed, Percy captured, 1,040 English were taken or left dead on the field and more were slain as they fled. The scots suffered only 100 dead and 200 prisoners. The dead, many with appalling head wounds were carried on:

> *. . . beeres*
> *Of byrch and haysell graye*

to Elsdon Church where they were buried.

The place where Douglas is reputed to have fallen is marked by a tall stone pillar, hidden in a small plantation of firs alongside the road between Otterburn and Greenchesters. For some reason the stone is called 'Percy's Cross'.

Twelve years later on Michaelmas Day the English gained a limited revenge for the bloody battle at Otterburn, when Sir Robert de Umfraville defeated another raiding party, and

> *Two hundreth men upon ye felde were slayne,*
> *Three hundreth fled, some hole some maymed sore*
> *That dyed at home with sorrows and wt payne,*
> *Some died homeward, yt home they came no more.*

John Hardyng, (1378–1465)

Percy's Cross

The Border Marches

As strife between the two nations increased, both Crowns made efforts to improve the administration and security of their own border lands by creating military zones called 'Marches'. By the mid-15th century the Border was lined by three pairs of opposing Marches: East, West and Middle, each under the supervision of a Warden. The original Wardens, *'Custodes Marchiarum'*, appointed in 1297 were professional soldiers but as the office gained in importance it became monopolised by the powerful feudal families in the area. The Warden's duties included liaising with his opposite number primarily to enforce the Border Laws, which were first documented in 1249. Regular meetings to settle disputes were held on an agreed day, 'The Day of the Law', at a mutually acceptable place. But even these days became occasions of fighting and vengeance.

One of the worst occurred on 7th July 1575 when a meeting was arranged at Redeswire between Sir John Forster, Warden of the Middle March (of which Redesdale was part) and Sir John Carmichael, Keeper of Liddesdale. At first the local disputes which came before them were settled amicably enough, but a great deal of heavy drinking was taking place and tempers grew more heated as the meeting progressed. On both sides there were those who bore mutual grudges so it was not long before fighting broke out, which Forster and Carmichael were unable to repress. In the scrimmage a number of the English were killed, among them the Deputy Warden, Sir George Heron. Forster himself, his son-in-law Lord Francis Russell (later to be killed at a Wardens' Meeting on Windygyle in Upper Coquetdale) and others, were seized and held prisoner for some time in Scotland. The affray, commemorated in the ballad 'The Raid of the Redeswire', may not have been a momentous event in the national politics of the day, but as far as international tensions on the Border were concerned, it was used as an excuse by the lairds and the kinships to intensify the 'deadlie fued'.

Kinships

The lairds were the heads of the main families or kinships in Redesdale. Each kinship was identified by a particular surname and strengthened by the system of inheritance known as 'gavelkind', by which a dead man's land was divided equally among all his sons.

In a 1551 report on the state of the Borders, Sir Robert Bowes observed the 'countrey of Riddesdalle standeth much by surnames, of which surnames the Haulls be the greatest and moste of the reputation in that countrey and next [to] them the Reades, Potts, Hedlies, Spoores, Dawgs and Fletchers'. Another kinship, a word still used in Redesdale, were the Andersons and, less numerous but more notorious, were the Coxons; the earliest reference to this family is in 1357 and the last, 1808. Another small but long established kinship were the Dunns; John Dunn of 'The Dunns' was to be murdered by reiving Scots in 1587. Close knit by blood ties each family united to its own advantage and for its own protection.

Feuds and Forays

The people of this countrey hath had one barbarous custom amongst them; if any two be displeased, they expect no law, but bang it out bravely, one and his kindred against the other, and his; they will subject themselves to no justice, but in an inhumane and barbarous manner, fight and kill one another; they run together [in] clangs (as they terme it) or names.

This fighting they call their feides, or deadly feides, a word so barbarous, that I cannot express it in any other tongue.

William Gray, 1649

Gray's graphic picture of a violent society on the borders in the 16th and early 17th centuries is one which has continually fired the imagination of romantic historians. Yet in all truth, the Borderers were nothing more than a delinquent minority who have subsequently acquired the aura of folk heroes. They lived in their own world of feud and foray, resenting not only the alien governments in London and Edinburgh who tried to control them but also the Border itself, which cut across their lands and their kinships. They were regarded as savages and unruly intruders by those who earned an honest living in the more settled areas of the North, especially Tyneside. The influential Merchant Adventurers of Newcastle, as mentioned earlier, refused to apprentice any youth who came from 'such lewde and wicked progenitors' as the inhabitants of Redesdale and Tynedale.

The root cause of all this wild behaviour was obvious even to contemporaries – there were simply too many mouths to feed and too little food and gainful employment to go round. Moreover, the population of Redesdale, estimated at about 4,000 was further increased by the garrison at Harbottle Castle, which had to be fed. Sir Robert Bowes recognised the problem as early as 1550, when he reported to the Marquis of Dorset, Lord Warden General, that 'there be more inhabitants than the said countries may sustain'. He went on to say that they would 'rather live poorly there as thieves than more wealthy in another countrey'.

Because there was not enough they took what they wanted by reiving, preying on both their neighbours and on rival kinships across the Border. 'These Highlanders are famous for thieving, they are all bred up and live by theft. They come down from these dales into the low countries, and carry away horses and cattell so cunningly, that it will be hard for any to get them or their cattell, except they be acquainted with some master thieves, who for some mony (which they call saufey mony) may help they to their stoln goods or receive them', wrote William Gray. The opening verses of the Ballad of the Death of Parcy Reed reflect the fear and resentment of the reivers:

> God send the land deliverance
> Frae every reaving, riding Scot,
> We'll sune hae neither cow nor ewe,
> We'll sune hae neither staig nor stot. (a young stallion and a young ox.)

That reiving was an established way of life is shown by a symbolic custom of the time. The laird's lady would bring to the table a trencher on which was a pair of spurs, to indicate that the larder was empty and would not be replenished until the menfolk had ridden out on another foray.

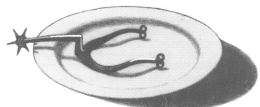

In 1581, the inhabitants of Rochester (now High Rochester) lodged a complaint before the Queen's Commissioners against the Elliots of Liddesdale, who had attacked on several occasions 'taking 180 kye and oxen, gotes, sheep and household stuff, so that the town has laid waste for 5 years'. In the same year in another raid by the Liddesdale men, this time on Elishaw, Ralph Hall was killed in his bed and in the pursuit 'was one Roger Wanles slayne, and his brother John, and two horses taken awaye'.

In 1584 Parcy Reed, the young Laird of Troughend, lost 200 cattle and 80 men prisoners with their horses and gear, in a foray by the Elliots, Croziers and others of Liddesdale, at Birdhope.

Amongst the bills presented at a Wardens' meeting at Alnwick on 6th April 1586, were complaints by William Coxon of Bagraw that Trissel of Merton and Robson of Middleknowes and others had stolen '12 kye and oxen and £3 worth of insight' in 1577.

The Redesdale men too played the reiving game. On 21st October 1583 the Laird of Cessford in a letter to Sir John Forster, Warden of the English Middle March, complained that 'the Halls of Gristounsteill (Girsonfield) has sum of my scheip, and sayis that they sall nocht want als long as I haif'.

Anyone, rich or poor, neighbour, compatriot or enemy, was fair game for the reivers, especially if a blood feud was involved. One of the prisoners confined in Newcastle Keep in 1621 was John Reed of Kelloburne (Kellyburn) whose family had a feud with the Delavals. Reed was charged with the 'felonius stealing of xxxte sheep and goodes of Edwarde Delavale of Alnwick Castle gent., and with the felonius stealing of ffower kyne the goodes of Rob'te Dalton of Welsled (Weetslade)'. He was also accused of reiving as far afield as 'the County of Yorke and Bishoprick of Durham'.

Cuddy of the Leam was sentenced at Newcastle Assize in 1628 to be sent to the wars (probably the Thirty Years War in Europe) with Captain Clark, for stealing a colt and breaking into the house of John Dunn of the Hillock.

The Wardens had only limited success in dealing with this endemic thieving. In 1518, ten of the biggest rogues in Redesdale were arrested by Thomas, Lord Dacre and imprisoned at Harbottle. They were subsequently rescued by their friends, who killed 6 of the 80-strong guard. Six years later a frustrated Dacre pleaded to be relieved of his office on the grounds of old age, debility and gout! In 1568 several Redesdale villains agreed to give themselves up at Harbottle Castle to answer charges brought against them by the Scottish Wardens. Once inside, noticing that the garrison was small, three of the rogues, all surnamed Hall, escaped. The rest were eventually overpowered. Four, amongst them Clement Hall of Birdhope, whose friends offered '9 score beasts for his life', were later beheaded at Morpeth.

Sometimes the Wardens themselves, and their deputy officers, actively encouraged or at least turned a blind eye to the outrages. Ralph Mansfield, Keeper of Redesdale under Lord Eure, Warden of the Middle March (1595–98) was accused by Elizabeth I's Commissioners of employing a notorious thief and murderer, George Hall of Birdhope, as a soldier in his Border patrols. Mansfield justified his action by stating that Sir Philip Sydney had asked Sir John Forster to allow Hall to live in Redesdale in recognition of his military service with him in the Netherlands. Even Forster himself was not above suspicion. There would be some truth in the statement that the felonies overlooked by Sir John Forster while he was Warden 'woulde fill a large booke'.

It is said that on awakening a Borderer would first feel his throat to make sure that it had not been slit in the night! Those involved in raiding were well aware that death was the penalty if they were caught, so every attack was carefully planned. A good horse was essential – not only to get the rider there, but more importantly to get him swiftly and safely home. The Borderers' horses, small, agile and sure-footed, were called hobblers or bog trotters. The raiders themselves were well equipped with a steel cap or bonnet, a jack (a light-weight quilted leather coat sewn with plates of metal or horn), leather breeches and boots, a lance, slashing sword, dagger and a heavy hand-gun, the 'dag'. Most

of the attacks were carried out at night, preferably when there was no moon. Total darkness was not a hazard, for riders knew every inch of the moors and mosses – hence their alternative name 'moss-troopers'. The high raiding season was from Michaelmas (29th September) to Martinmas (11th November) when the fells were 'good and drie and cattle strong to dryve'. It was also easier to rustle beasts which were grazing on 'wintersteeds', (the land nearest the settlement), than to attempt to gather them up from the high, open shieling grounds during the summer.

The size of the raiding parties varied. One of the largest recorded is that of 3,000 Scots against the English Middle March in 1532. Forays were much less ambitious. They were made by groups of 50–100 men on smaller and more localised targets. Although the prime object of the raid was to procure meat on the hoof, the robbers also took anything else they could lay their hands on from inside peoples' houses – 'insight gear', and outside – 'outsight gear'. In about 1594 the Scottish Laird of Makerston served a bill upon Michael, alias Hogg Skynnes Hedley of Hatherwick, for taking 'a pistol worth 40s; 1 sword 10s; a steel cap 10s; a handkerchief 5s; a scarf 2s; his purse containing a rose noble and other mony 24s; a pair of worsted stockings 10s; a cloak 13s 4d and his silk garters 3s.' He was obviously a worthy target. With forays from Liddesdale averaging one per week by the late 1580s it comes as no surprise that the total value of cattle and goods taken in Redesdale over the period 1577–1586 was estimated at £12,394, while the number of tenancies destroyed between 1583 and 1586 was 1,157.

The Solution to these Problems ....

'As soon as they have seized upon the booty, they, in like manner return home in the night.' There were 40 passages through the Middle March, 23 of them by way of the Rede valley, so the authorities had little hope of catching the thieves. Whilst the monarchs of both nations accepted that something had to be done to cure this running sore, Border affairs were not the main concern of central government in the 16th century. The easiest solution was to give the Wardens additional powers to deal with the cross-Border strife. The number of Deputy Wardens and Warden-Sergeants for each Warden was increased from two to four and a new office, that of Keeper, was created. The offices of Keeper and Warden-Sergeant were sometimes given to local lairds who, it was felt, would be able to exert a restraining influence over the more wayward characters in their kinships.

In 1526 John Hall of Otterburn was required to serve Henry VIII with six horse-men for which he was paid an annual fee of 20 marks, and in 1540 in recognition of his loyalty he was made a pensioner of the Crown. His son, also John Hall, was appointed Sergeant of Redesdale and Tynedale in 1552 and had 50 light horsemen, all of his own surname, to keep order.

But there were some who were jealous and resentful of those who were offered high office, not least the 'fause-hearted Ha's of Girsonfield'. For long enough they had had a 'deadlie feud' with the Reeds of Troughend and when Parcy Reed became Keeper of Redesdale, the Halls were greatly disgruntled. In the course of his duties as official upholder of Elizabeth's Border Laws, Reed arrested and brought to trial a Crozier from Liddesdale. The lad's father swore revenge on Reed and was offered help by the Halls. They persuaded Parcy to join them for a day's hunting (his favourite occupation) near Carter Bar, ensured that he was tired by his exertions and then suggested that they all should have a rest. When Reed fell asleep, the Halls poured water into his gun, rammed his sword fast in its scabbard and then abandoned him to the Croziers who were hiding nearby:

> They fell upon him all at once,
> They mangled him most cruellie;
> The slightest wound might caused his deid,
> And they hae gien him thirty-three;
> They hacket off his hands and feet,
> And left him lying on the lee.

Poor Parcy's corpse was so badly mutilated that the remains had to be carried in sacks to Troughend! His ghost is reputed to haunt the Bateinghope valley where the ghastly murder took place and the banks of the Rede, in particular near the ruins of Todlaw Mill. In another local tale, a thatcher busy on the roof of Woolaw, saw the ghost, had the temerity to speak to it, then immediately died of fright!

Since the most difficult task of the wardens on both sides of the Border was to make sure that the criminal elements in the population were 'continually in dread of justice under their keepers', days of truce or 'March days' were held regularly at mutually accceptable places. The Meetings of the Middle March Wardens were held near busy cross-Border routes – places which are very remote now. The normal meeting place for the Rede valley people was not the Redeswire, where the A68 crosses the Border, for in the sixteenth century the main route into Scotland was still the old Roman road of Dere Street, so the Warden Meeting took place close to the Roman staging post of Chew Green at the head of Coquetdale. At the Meeting the Wardens produced their prisoners – those that is who had not taken 'leg-bail' by fleeing to another district! Complainants also presented bills against offenders for redress of grievances.

The March Laws adhered to by all the Wardens were of necessity severe. Fines for stealing beasts ranged from 2 shillings for a young goat to 6 shillings for an old sheep and 30 shillings for a cow more than 4 years old. The death penalty was imposed for a number of offences which included marrying a woman from over the Border without the Warden's permission, selling weapons, bread, corn, horses, forging coin of the realm, harbouring fugitives and accepting protection or 'saufey' money. Death was either by hanging, beheading or, a method favoured by the Scots, drowning in the nearest burn.

More often than not it was impossible to catch the culprits. Even when they were captured charges were hard to prove unless the villains had been caught red-handed. In 1552 a system of setters and searchers was established along the entire Border to watch every conceivable route which the reivers might take day and night from October to mid-March. Some of the most vulnerable places in Redesdale were the two fords at Garretshiels, the two fords at Elishaw and the ford at Todlaw. Those who lived nearest had to provide the setters and the searchers of the watches. This system was not infallible for some of the watchers undoubtedly would be in league with the raiders. Additional surveillance was provided by mobile patrols furnished by local men or detachments sent out from the main garrison at Harbottle. If sufficient warning was received, the Warden was empowered by an Act of 1563 'to pursue and chase in hot-trod unto such time or place as the fugitives be apprehended'. Accordingly he mustered all able-bodied men between the ages of 16 and 60, mounted and armed in keeping with their status, to chase 'with hound and horn, hue and cry' and bearing on the tip of their lances a burning piece of turf. The hounds known as 'slewdogges' were probably the forbears of the keen-scented trail hounds of today. They were valuable, highly-prized by their owners and not infrequently stolen by the reivers.

Successes were rare and there were times when the frustrated Wardens resorted to punitive measures. In 1544, Sir Ralph Evers crossed the Border, burnt Kelso and Jedburgh to the ground and plundered the surrounding countryside destroying towns, towers, farmsteads, barmkins, parish churches, bastle houses; he killed 400 people and made off with 816 prisoners, 10,386 cattle, 12,496 sheep, 200 goats, 850 bolls of corn and 'insight gear – an indefinite quantity'. Even such horrific measures as this were to no avail, for the system of plunder and retaliation grew more intense as the 16th century progressed. The wardens lacked the men, horses and money to cope with 'this gangrene'; central government lacked the interest.

The End of the Liberty of Redesdale

The lairds and the kinships cannot be held solely responsible for all the strife on the Anglo-Scottish frontier; the rival Crowns must accept some of the blame since they deliberately exploited the explosive situation in order to weaken each other's authority. On the other hand, neither Crown could allow the growing independence of the Redesdale lairds to go unchallenged. Before any attempt could be made to restore stability on the Border, the power of the lairds and their patrons, the Border barons, would have to be broken. Fate this time was on the side of the monarch. When the last male heir of the Umfravilles died childless in 1437, the Lordship reverted to a cousin, Sir Walter Taylbois (Talbot) of Hepple. One hundred years later, Henry VIII acquired Redesdale from Elizabeth, sister of the last Lord Taylbois, and he used his opportunity to deprive the Liberty of many of its ancient privileges and bring it under the jurisdiction of the Sheriff of Northumberland.

Elizabeth I's most effective measure to deal with the problems of the area was to dismiss the Earl of Northumberland from the Wardenship of the Middle March in 1559 and give the post to Sir John Forster, a lowland Northumbrian, who had no vested interest in the area. In his 36 years as Warden, Forster employed outsiders as his officials in Redesdale. He destroyed the homes of those who were likely to cause trouble, took some of the lairds hostage for the good behaviour of their kinships, secretly encouraged the Scots to raid, burn settlements, drive off beasts and horses and exact heavy ransoms for the large number of prisoners they captured. By the end of the 16th century, not one able-bodied man in the valley could provide his own horse and weapons to ride with the Warden in defence of the Border. And by that time Sir John was a very unpopular old man.

What finally brought about the demise of reiving was the succession of James VI of Scotland to the throne of England in 1603, thus uniting the Crowns. Twelve days after his arrival in England he declared that his aim was to achieve union between the two kingdoms and to bring the Borderers to heel under the rule of law. He therefore forbade the use of the word 'Borders', substituting in its place the name 'Middle Shire'. All strongholds except those of noblemen were to be demolished, their iron gates converted to ploughshares and every inhabitant was to turn his hand to peaceful pursuits – another central government Diktat which came to nought! It did *not* bring an immediate end to reiving, but rather as national prejudices and local feuds gradually died out in the 17th century, so reiving also declined and with it the once powerful hold of the lairds and the kinships. Those who for long had been a cut-throat brotherhood became, under the increasing influence of the Church and education, part of an honest, diligent, God-fearing (but not necessarily sober) community.

And what of the Liberty and the Lordship? In 1604 it was once more granted to a subject, this time to James I's favourite George Home, Earl of Dunbar. In 1613 it passed to Dunbar's daughter, Elizabeth, and her husband, Lord Howard of Walden, on payment of £72 12s 4d, 4lb of pepper and 1lb of cumin, both valuable spices. The Howard family held the estate until 1750 when financial difficulties forced William Howard to sell the Manor of Redesdale, the patronage of Elsdon church and the farm of Overacres to Hugh, first Duke of Northumberland. The total annual value of all this property was now only £350! Summer pasturing grounds at the head of the valley had already changed ownership in the 17th century and further land transactions during the 18th and 19th centuries led eventually to the extinction of the old Liberty of Redesdale.

The present title 'Lord Redesdale' is held by the Mitford family and dates back to 1802, when Sir John Mitford was created Baron Redesdale.

The Legacy of the Feuds & Forays

An' aye we sang o' the old times,
An' monie a tale we tauld
Of Tyne and Reed and Liddesdale,
An' moss-troopers sae bauld;
Of midnight raid, an' morning fight,
By grey peel, cairn or stream,
Till fancy heard the slogan wild,
An' saw the bright steel gleam.

James Armstrong, 1879

Bastles and Ballads

A reminder of the raids of Border reivers is the survival into the present of defensible farmhouses known as bastles. The origin of the word 'bastle' is probably a corruption of the French 'bastille', meaning 'a small fortress'. One of the earliest uses of the word in English occurs in 1544, when Sir Ralph Evers, Warden of the Middle March (1537–45) mentioned 'bastells' in the list of buildings destroyed by his men in a foray into the Scottish Lowlands.

Bastles were not impregnable, but it took time to break into the ground floor, drive off the beasts and smoke out the defenders. As these farmhouses were frequently sited within 3 or 4km and often within sight of each other, news of a raid would quickly spread and bring help from neighbours, who on another occasion might themselves require similar assistance.

Cut away view of typical Bastle – Living quarters above animals below. The steps replace the earlier ladder.

27

Bastles are found only in a belt 33km wide, extending the length of the Anglo-Scottish Border, and nowhere else in Britain. The reason is that this was the limit of a defensive zone established by the English Crown in 1555 to deter the reivers. Those who lived in this area were required to dig ditches and set hedges to hinder the passage of the mounted raiders. Few of the recommendations made by four government inquiries into the state of the Borders were acted upon, so there was no provision for the defence of the population who were forced to fend for themselves. The more wealthy farmers, perhaps the lairds of the kinships, built bastles, whilst the poor, accepting the inevitable, constructed their homes of turf which, if not providing the best accommodation, at least could be rebuilt quickly after a raid.

It was not until the Restoration of 1660 and a return to more settled political conditions generally, that bastles ceased to serve as defensible farmhouses. Many were subsequently modified; for instance external stone stairs replaced the movable wooden ladder which originally gave access to the upper floor. They continued to be used as farmhouses, or as the nuclei of small farming communities until well into the 18th and 19th centuries; some, such as Raw near Elsdon are now used as farm outbuildings.

Ironhouse Bastle 1978

Border Ballads

The most enduring legacy of the feuds and forays are the Border ballads. Composed by unknown ballad-makers, these narratives were passed down orally by hill shepherds and their families, until by the end of the 18th century the increased use of the printed word led to a decline in the tradition of ballad singing. Many of the tales must have been lost, but that some have survived is mainly due to the efforts of Sir Walter Scott. His intense interest in Border history induced him to record them in his 'Border Minstrelsy' (1802–3) and to popularise them with his own composition 'The Lay of the Last Minstrel'.

The ballads recount local incidents and events which made a great impact on the imagination of the Border communities. The accounts may not necessarily be accurate or impartial, but they reflect to some degree the personal allegiances of the composers. The ballad didn't just tell a good story; it was also a propaganda vehicle. Some glorified the kinships and their warlike activities, some decried them. Thus loyalty and hospitality were commended, treachery and betrayal, as depicted in 'The Death of Parcy Reed', were bitterly denounced. The particular branch of the Halls who took part in the deed were forced to leave Redesdale for ever. Blood, love and tragedy were the essential components of the ballads; so too was rough humour, found for instance in the tales of 'Jock o' the Side', 'Johnnie Armstrong' and 'Hobie Noble', which made heroes out of the reivers. On the other hand several ballads, notably 'Rookhope Ride', sympathise with the ordinary folk, who suffered most in the conflicts whilst only wanting to be left in peace. It is lucky for us that from the apparently unpromising background of the patriarchal kinship there should emerge a few poets who, with their word pictures, could reveal to later ages the manners and way of life of their own times.

Elsdon, a Frontier Town

If ye've niver been at Elsdon,
Take ma advice and gan,
For ivery chiel in Elsdon,
Is ivery inch a man.
Ay, there's decent folk in Elsdon,
As iver aw did see,
So aw'm away to Elsdon,
And come alang wi' me.

Anon.

Although the great stone castle at Harbottle was the stronghold of the Lords of Redesdale and the Wardens of the Middle March, their capital was Elsdon. The massive Norman earthwork on the Mote Hills, St Cuthbert's Church, the Pele Tower and the development of the village round the green give some idea of Elsdon's importance in medieval times.

Popular tradition has it that Elsdon derived its name from Elli, a fierce and cruel giant who lived on the Mote Hills. More probably, Elsdon has its origins in the late Anglian period, as Elli's denu or dene, an outpost on the north west fringe of Northumbria. Unlike the scattered hill-top settlements of the Romano-British farmers and their descendants, Elsdon was a relatively compact community at first. Secure behind the bounds of a high hedge or fence, its timber houses bordered a central grassy area where livestock could be driven at night or in times of danger. After the Norman Conquest, when Elsdon achieved the status of a Township, this open space, which now covers 3 hectares, became the Toon Green or Common.

Elsdon

Elsdon Fair

It was here that the weekly Thursday market and three-day annual fair on 24th, 25th and 26th August were held in accordance with Edward I's charter granted to William de Umfraville in 1281. Every year the Lord's Steward urged the townsfolk to preserve the peace 'without offering any violence, making Raid, Rout or unlawful assembly, drawing any weapons or spilling blood during the continuance of this present Fair'. Looking at the green now it is hard to imagine the bustle, the excitement, the shouts of the traders, the sight and smell of cattle and horses, while all manner of other goods from cheese, butter, brushwood, animal skins, grease and spices, to iron nails, griddles, pots, horse-shoes and hemp were for sale. Both the market and the fair are now extinct. The fair died out about 1870, but the weekly market had already long ceased to function. Writing to his patron the Duke of Northumberland in 1762, the Rev C. Dodgson, newly appointed Rector of Elsdon, remarked 'Most certain it is that the oldest man in the parish never saw a market here in his life'.

The Common was also the setting for more sinister events – the punishment of wrong doers. The place where trials took place is uncertain but the jurors, who were all local men, had to consider not only criminal offences but also to report on rents or services withheld from the Lord, the removal of boundaries, the illegal use of hunting dogs, the repair of the pillory and pinfold and to supervise the election of ale and bread tasters. The gallows and the pillory served as grim reminders of the Lord's power and provided public entertainment as well. Another spectacle on the green was the Midsummer bonfire through which all cattle were driven to ward off disease and the influence of the Evil Eye. The gallows and the pillory have long since vanished from the village. The pinfold is still there and also the grass-grown hollow which once was the cockpit, where feathers flew and wagers were laid as spurred champions crowed and fought, to the delight of the onlookers. But it is the grey sandstone church of St Cuthbert, the 'Cathedral of the Rede', which is now the main attraction for the visitor.

The original foundation of the church is obscure, but legend has it that the first church was erected over the place where St Cuthbert's coffin rested briefly in AD 875 during the monks' wanderings around Northumbria after their flight from Lindisfarne. The present building dates mainly from the 14th century, but earlier architecture is preserved in the narrowness of the aisles and transepts, in the 12th century pilasters and in the small, round arched 13th century windows. In the 17th century a little bell-turret was added. This did not meet with the approval of the Rev Dodgson who described it to his patron as 'an Elsdonic kind of cupola and the only bell which is in it is almost as loud as that which calls your Lordship's labourers to dinner at Sion House. It may be heard at the Castle when the wind is favourable.' During the restoration work of 1837 a box containing the skulls of three horses was found in a cavity in the tiny spire which tops the belfry – rather reminiscent of the old pagan practice of sacrificing valued animals or even infants when a new building was dedicated. So even though the bell was hung in the 17th century pagan practices may have survived in the area long after such beliefs were officially regarded by the Church as comfortably extinct.

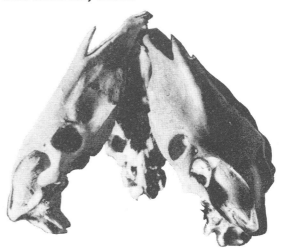

*Sword marks on pillar
in Elsdon Church*

Many things in St Cuthbert's bring the people of the past vividly to life. The grooves worn in the pillars nearest the entrance are where 'the wild men of Redesdale' sharpened their knives and swords before setting out on their business. A resourceful stonemason working on the entrance used two stone coffin lids to form the lintel; one of them is engraved with a Celtic cross and a pair of shears. The parish register dating back to 1672 records the arrivals and departures of the parishioners and provides a fascinating glimpse into the life of Elsdon, as the following extracts show:

29 Mch 1669	Geo. Anderson jnr. of Birdop Cragg for a birth not given notis of but as wee hear.
6 Aug 1741	James and John ss *(sons)* of Wm Dunn of Hole Miln, drowned, bur.
16 Mch 1751	Mary, d *(daughter)* Robert and Barbara Trotter of Rattenraw, dissenters, born.
2 Mch 1802	James Brown; labourer, accidentally killed in a slate quarry by a fall of stone, aged 36.

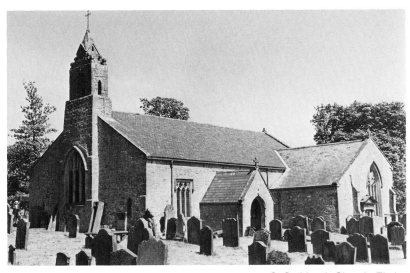

St Cuthbert's Church, Elsdon

Inside the church are a number of monumental slabs commemorating former Rectors, and members of important local families: the Halls, Reeds, Andersons and Hedleys. One bears the arms of the Umfravilles. There is also a Roman tombstone, brought from the fort of High Rochester in 1809. The inscription records Rufinus, a tribune of the 3rd century garrison, the Vardullorum. He died at the age of 48½ years and the tombstone was set up by his wife, Iulia Lucilla. Probably some of the stone used to build the church was also robbed from High Rochester.

The north wall of St Cuthbert's has shallower foundations than the rest of the building. In the late 14th century, workers involved in construction unearthed the remains, not entirely decomposed, of men in their prime, lying close together in a communal grave. Not wishing to disturb this grisly interment, the masons built the north wall over the bones. Further evidence of this mass grave was found during restoration work in 1810 and in 1877; it is probably the last resting place for the dead of the Battle of Otterburn.

Elsdon Tower, or Pele, lies just north of the church, perched high above the steep-sided ravine cut by the Elsdon Burn. It is now privately owned, but before the comfortable adjoining house was built in the early 19th century, it was the cold and draughty residence of the vicars of Elsdon – a fortified parsonage, like Corbridge Pele.

The Sands of Time . . . at Elsdon

Elsdon Pele

As a first defence, there was a barmkin round the tower, into which livestock could be driven for protection. This is now a carefully tended garden. The walls of the tower are as much as 3m thick in places with a spiral staircase built into them. This winds up to the left, to give the defender the unrestricted use of his sword arm. An additional aid to defence here is the cunningly placed trip-step, higher than the rest to unbalance the rash invader. Steeply-gabled against the rigours of the climate, the present roof replaces the original level area enclosed by crenellated battlements, from behind which it was possible to view the surrounding countryside with some degree of safety.

Outside, high up on the south wall of the tower, is the heraldic shield of the Umfravilles; the Lord of Redesdale's right of tenure is represented by the supporters – wolves, each of which bears a sword. The inscription reads . . .

R. Dominus de Rede

The 'R' probably refers to Robert de Umfraville, who held the Lordship from 1390 to 1436. He was nicknamed Robin Mend-Market from the vast quantity of beasts and food which he stole on his raids into Scotland, and which he re-sold in Northumberland at lower prices than those charged in the local markets.

There was probably an earlier building here to accommodate the first-recorded rector, Vincent Cornwallis, 1245, and his successors, but the present pele was built in the 14th century. Daily life in the Tower must have been cold, damp, dirty and smoky. The Rev Dodgson did not mince his words:

The vestibule of the Castle is a low stable, and above it is the kitchen in which there are two little beds joining to each other. The curate and his wife lay in one, and Margery, the maid, in the other. I lay in the parlour, between two beds, to keep me from being frozen to death, for, as we keep open house, the winds enter from every quarter, and are apt to creep into bed to one.

This particular rector did not stay long in Elsdon – he endured it for three years, then left.

The Lords of Redesdale were probably just as uncomfortable in their first residence. Situated on a spur overlooking the Elsdon Burn, the Mote Hills is one of the finest examples of a motte and bailey castle in England. This early Norman earthwork built c.1080 dominates the village and was the Umfravilles' administrative centre until they installed themselves in Harbottle castle about fifty years later. The builders created the defences of their stronghold out of a huge deposit of glacial drift. The circular motte, on which they built a timber castle, is about 15m high, flat-topped and protected by a deep ditch. A rectangular courtyard or bailey, ringed by a massive earth bank and an outer ditch, adjoins the north side. To appreciate the scale of this dramatic structure and the amount of effort which went into making it, take the minor road towards Scots Gap, and stop at the scenic layby on Battle Hill.

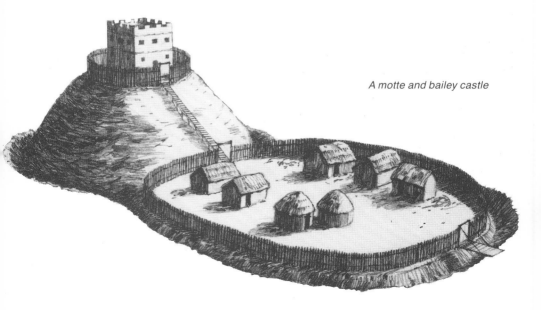

A motte and bailey castle

There is a gallows or gibbet at the top of this hill and a head swings from it in the wind. In reality it is a wooden replica of the head of William Winter, a man of villainous stock. Both his father and brother had been hanged at Morpeth in 1788. Four years later at Raw Bastle, Winter and his accomplices Jane and Eleanor Clark, murdered an old woman, Margaret Crozier, in the mistaken belief that she was rich. All three were caught near Stamfordham and convicted on the evidence of a shepherd boy, who had seen them skulking in a sheepfold on Whiskershiels Common. After their execution, Winter's body was hung in chains from the gibbet erected near Steng Cross, an old boundary stone, in view of the scene of his crime. The body eventually disintegrated, but the wooden head, hung in its stead, is a melancholy sight even on a bright summer's day. Long after the event 'Winter's Stob' was a place of pilgrimage, particularly for the villagers of Stamfordham. It was said the 'pilgrims' believed that chips of wood from the gibbet were, when rubbed over the gums, a sure cure for toothache!

Elsdon was relatively unaffected by all this past drama. Despite its status as the civil and ecclesiastical centre of the Liberty of Redesdale, its communications were poor and as a result it never grew into a town. George Chatt, the Hexham poet, scathingly described Elsdon as 'the world's unfinished neuk'. For many centuries the village remained isolated. The construction of the turnpike road from Belsay to Otterburn during the 1830s came too late to encourage expansion and anyway it by-passed the village by one mile. The demand during the Agricultural Revolution for locally produced coal and lime did however contribute to a brief period of prosperity. The population increased to about 300 by the mid-19th century and property was improved; the cottages on the east side of the Green, the former Presbyterian Meeting House, Bacchus Inn, Rector's School and the Bird in Bush Inn, all date from that period.

But fifty years later foreign agricultural competition and the decline of the rural industries put many out of work. The population began to drift away. Although the slump was temporarily halted at the turn of the 20th century with the development of Elsdon Colliery, the mine eventually ceased production in 1972. The Rector's School closed in 1974, the rector himself having lived at Otterburn since 1962.

Elsdon is 48km from Newcastle, a mere 50 minutes drive from a conurbation of over one million people. Yet the village has remained free from those modern transformations which some believe have destroyed the character of so many English villages in recent years. That Elsdon has been usurped as Redesdale's ancient capital by Hodgson's 'emporium' Otterburn is a fact, but as the historic centre of Redewater, Elsdon's claim cannot be denied.

Religion

Another most grievous decay is 'want of knowledge of God'.

Ralph, Lord Eure, 1596

'In Redesdale be three parish churches. The chiefest is Ellesdene.' When Henry VIII's antiquary John Leland made this statement England's church was still under the rule of Rome. Elsdon parish, 310 sq km of wild countryside in the Archdeaconry of Northumberland, presented considerable problems for the rector of St Cuthbert's, not least in the hazards of both climate and terrain. The inconveniences they experienced must also have discouraged the authorities in Durham from making many visitations to this remote part of the diocese. Only rarely was interest shown in the activities of the local priests. In 1498 Bishop Fox, who took his role more seriously than most, denounced the clergy in Redesdale and Tynedale as 'publicly and openly living with concubines . . . and wholly ignorant of letters, so much so, that priests of ten years did not know how to read the ritual. Some of them are even nothing more than sham priests, having never been ordained.' Twenty five years later the commissioners for the management of affairs on the Borders informed Cardinal Wolsey, the Papal Legate, that they had been forced to close the churches in Tynedale because there was so much wickedness there, but they had refrained from imposing similar measures in Redesdale because 'it is metely well rewled'·

It is not known how strongly entrenched Catholicism was in Redesdale. No great abbeys were founded there in medieval times; the nearest Houses were those across the Border in Jedburgh and Melrose. There were no large Catholic estates to sustain the faith during the religious upheavals of the 16th century. So in the 1569 Rebellion of the Northern Earls, which unsuccessfully attempted to restore Catholicism in place of the Protestant Church of England, the Borders remained quiet.

After England turned to the protestant faith, it seems that the few Borderers who still clung to Catholicism were of the gentry. Some were allowed to hold public office under Elizabeth I and continued to do so, even after such posts were forbidden to them after the Gunpowder Plot in 1605. The Howards, to whom James I sold the Lordship of Redesdale, were Catholics; so too was Edward Grey of Morpeth, Deputy Warden of the Middle March in 1597 and later a member of the first Border Commission. Another local Catholic was Sir Henry Widdrington. He was Deputy Warden of the Middle March in 1601 and thrice MP for Northumberland from 1604 until his death in 1623; this despite the fact that James' Commissioners had noted in 1607 that he was married to Mary Currien, sister of a 'Cumberland Papist' and that he 'cometh seldom to

Church'. But records show that Government fears were unwarranted; of the total population of 83,000 in Northumberland in the early 17th century, probably less than 2 per cent were Catholics.

In Redesdale, those Catholics who remained true to their faith were left in a state of religious isolation. Their only hope of spiritual nourishment was by the ministrations of the occasional priest from the Continent who landed secretly on the Northumberland coast and passed through the area by safe houses, on his way to more important centres of Catholicism further south. The tower house at Corsenside probably provided one of these sanctuaries; a tiny room has been discovered built into the thickness of the south wall, and this seems to have been a priests' hole.

Emancipation in 1829 presented Catholics with an opportunity to revive their faith. A hundred years later they were offered the use of a barn on Granny Brydon's farm at West Townhead, Otterburn. This served as a place of worship until St. Peter's, the only Catholic church in the Rede valley, was built in Otterburn in 1955.

The Anglican Church established in 1559 by Elizabeth I, fared little better at first than the Catholic Church, mainly because it was starved of money. Elizabeth, perenially hard up, often sold small country livings, together with the right to appoint the priest and collect the tithes, to secular landowners who usually failed to maintain the building or to pay the vicar a decent living wage.

In 1663, when John Hall of Otterburn was the lay patron of the 'chappell of Corsonside', the living was only worth £7 15s 4d – well below its real value. The vicar John Graham, who had been the incumbent for 46 years, was paid a meagre stipend of £16 13s 4d per annum. Small wonder that he wore 'tatter'd weeds' and was 'sordid and worn to the bones by sharp misery'. Even Elsdon Church, whose patronage still rested in the hands of the Bishop of Durham, was destitute. Hugh Farrington, Rector in 1733, had to take Gabriel Hall of Catcleugh 'and others' to court at the Newcastle Assize for non-payment of a tithe of hay and corn. It seems that the Rector's job was a constant struggle for survival, but he did have one unusual perquisite: in the days before the parish had a hearse, the dead were carried to the graveside on a bier of poles, called 'pike handles'. When the corpse had been laid to rest, the Rector could claim the 'pike handles'. Many clergy were reluctant to accept the Elsdon living because they were afraid for their personal safety. 'In this rude, superstitious people on the Borders, priests go with sword, dagger and such apparel as they can get' wrote Pilkington, who was Bishop of Durham from 1561–1578.

There were some however who regarded Redesdale and its wild inhabitants as a personal challenge, amongst them Bernard Gilpin, the incumbent of Houghton-le-Spring in Durham and self-styled 'Apostle of the North'. Gilpin's visits to Redesdale were made annually and always at Christmas, the one time of the year that the 'half barbarous and rustic people' made an effort to come to church. If there was a church, he preached in it, if not, in a barn or any other suitable building. 'In his sermons he spoke very plainly to his hearers of the wicked and careless lives they were leading and explained to them what real godliness was.' In the course of his mission Gilpin, accompanied by his servant William Airey, endured great physical hardships of cold and hunger. 'The country was so poor that what provision he could get, extreme hunger only could make palatable', wrote his descendant William Gilpin. There was danger too. Once his horses were stolen, to be returned later by the repentant thief. On another occasion, as he was leaving a church in Redesdale he saw a bloody hand impaled on a spear. This was a recognised sign for a fight to the death between two enemies. Gilpin 'got some of the better sort of the country to join with him, and after some pains made up the quarrel'.

Whether Gilpin's crusading zeal had much long term effect on the Redesdale populace is doubtful; given the instability of the area, religion would not have been the first concern of its inhabitants. Sir William Bowes admitted in 1595 that in the Middle March 'true religion has taken very little place', a statement underlined by Sir Benjamin Rudyard in 1628, when he informed the House of Commons that 'in the utmost skirts of the North where the Prayers of the common people are more like spells and Charms than devotions, God is little better known than amongst the Indians'.

This spiritual vacuum was filled by men of other religious persuasions, who themselves were seeking sanctuary in the Borders – Protestant Nonconformists or Dissenters opposed to the authority claimed by the Anglican Bishops. Following Charles I's execution in 1649, Nonconformists gained religious freedom for a while under Cromwell, while Catholics and Anglicans were discouraged. But with the Restoration of Charles II in 1660, Nonconformists experienced an era of persecution which was particularly vicious in Scotland. Of the 2,000 ministers ejected from their livings for refusal to comply with the Act of Uniformity and be re-ordained by Bishops, the majority were Scottish Presbyterians or Covenanters. A number of them sought refuge in the Borders, where they continued their ministry in defiance of the authorities. Forbidden to preach within 8km of any town, the Presbyterians held their meetings or Conventicles secretly, on lonely hillsides or wherever the landscape would conceal them from the watchful eyes of those who tried to betray them. Chattlehope (or Babswood Kirk), a cave near Catcleugh, Deadwood Kirk, a clearing in a wood of oak and birch near Birdhope and Huel (Holy) Kirk, a natural bowl amongst rocky crags near the Sills Burn, are all traditionally associated with the Covenanters.

Two fugitive ministers, Alexander Peden (1626–1686) and William Veitch (1640–1722) were mainly responsible for the spiritual regeneration of the local population. Peden, a diminutive figure with lank hair, sallow complexion, dark, penetrating eyes and a shrill squeaking voice was nevertheless a gifted orator. He also had prophetic powers and endured great hardships which enhanced his reputation still more. He often preached on a hill, now called Padon Hill, near Gibshiel and a stone cairn marks the site where he held his services. Peden's Well at the foot of Birdhopecraig was another of his preaching places. The authorities eventually caught up with him north of the Border and he was imprisoned for five years on the Bass Rock in the Firth of Forth. William Veitch also spent an enforced period there. Outlawed in 1667, he too fled to Northumberland, preaching under the assumed name of 'Mr. Johnson'.

Veitch was active in Redesdale until 1677 and had some narrow escapes from the militia. On one occasion he avoided capture on Carter Bar by hiding in a bothy, so cunningly constructed with heather and turf that it seemed one with its surroundings. In 1685 in the mistaken belief that he had considerable support in Northumberland, he unsuccessfully tried to raise the county against the succession of the Catholic King, James II.

At considerable risk to themselves, the heads of the Redesdale kinships sometimes offered their houses as meeting places. In 1669 John Hall of Otterburn, the same man who held the patronage of the Anglican church at Corsenside, was reported for holding Conventicles.

Corsenside Church

41

After James II was ousted by William of Orange in 1688, persecution ceased and religious attitudes mellowed considerably. By 1762, the Rev Dodgson commented that 'Those who live near Elsdon come to church – those at a greater distance towards the west go to the Meeting House at Birdhope Craig – others both Churchmen and Presbyterians, at any great distance go to the nearest church or Conventical in a neighbouring parish. There is a very good understanding between the parties, for they not only intermarry with one another, but frequently do penance together in a white sheet, with a white wand, barefoot in the coldest season of the year.'

Birdhopecraig is probably one of the oldest Nonconformist Meetings in Northumberland. Although there is some doubt about the actual date of foundation, it is known that shortly after William III took the throne, the Presbyterians met in a house on Birdhopecraig and that before 1720 at least three Ministers had accepted the call to serve. In 1826 a new Meeting House and a manse were erected on a plot of land at Sillsburnfoot and a school was provided in 1840. Meeting houses at Otterburn and Spithopehaugh, higher up the valley, were founded for isolated congregations.

Birdhopecraig Manse and Kirk – under flood

Diary from Birdhopecraig

gregation also acting Elder in Thropton Con also as the Assembly meets in the middle of the Lambing Season when it is impossible for any of our own Elders to attend the Moderator was authorized to give Communion to any bona fide act of the Church

Rev. Newlands

Other Nonconformist sects were less successful in Redesdale and neither Quaker nor Methodist meeting places survive.

After several centuries of apparent apathy, the Anglican Church awoke to its responsibilities towards its more isolated parishioners. At the instigation of the Rev Dodgson's successor, Louis Dutens, Byrness Chapel was built in what Hodgson describes as an 'ancient burial ground'. Erected in 1793 by voluntary subscription, it cost £1,750 to which the Rev Dutens, obviously a man of more affluence than many of his predecessors, contributed two-thirds of the total. The Chapel, now the Church of St Francis, was once the smallest in the Diocese; it measures approximately 8.5m by 5.5m. A stained-glass window depicts workers employed on the construction of Catcleugh Reservoir. The window is dedicated to 60 men, women and children who died of cholera while work was in progress in the late 1890s.

Byrness Church

In 1844, the lovely church of Holy Trinity was built at Horsley and on 28 September 1855 the foundation stone of St John's Otterburn was laid. Designed by the famous Newcastle architect John Dobson this Church was the gift of private benefactors.

The Three R's

As teaching children to read their Mother Tongue is of great importance to Society, surely every attempt to facilitate that laudable employment cannot fail of being acceptable to the public.

Thomas Hastie, Schoolmaster, 1799

Initially it was the law and influence of the Church, particularly the Presbyterian Church, which tempered the 'desperate banditti' of Redesdale. Education was slow to reach the valley and when it did, in the 18th and 19th centuries, it was mainly through the agency of the Anglican Church and the generosity of noble benefactors.

This is not to say that in earlier centuries everyone was uneducated. For those who had the inclination and the wealth, it was possible to gain some learning elsewhere. The will of Gabriel Hall of Ottercops, dated 14 April 1563, makes provision for his sons Edward and Nicholas to be sent to school in Newcastle and 'when they have learned that there frends thinks to be done in lernings and understandinge, each to have £20 to make a stock of merchandise'.

In the 17th century when the Borders became more peaceful, Newcastle merchants were once again prepared to apprentice a number of Redesdale 'callants'. Many of them did well in their chosen trade, amongst them Edward

Anderson of Birdhopecraig. Apprenticed to James Hargrave, a Newcastle mercer, he was 'admitted to the freedom of the Merchant Adventurers Company' in 1705 and when he died in 1725, was buried in St Nicholas' Cathedral. However, the ordinary folk of Redesdale had to wait until well into the 18th century before they had any chance of schooling.

The first schools in the valley were run by itinerant and often unqualified schoolmasters, although some were literate clergymen. Permanent schools followed later, once local interest had been roused.

One of the earliest schoolmasters seems to have been John Dinning, whose gravestone at Corsenside states that he had been schoolmaster in Elsdon and Corsenside from 1731–1781. The interest of local worthies is shown by the will of Cuthbert Fenwick, who in 1748 left 10 shillings to provide teaching for the children of Elsdon, but it was only in 1835 that a proper school was built by the rector, Archdeacon Thomas Singleton. By 1939, the decline of rural industries based in the Elsdon area had speeded up a population decline, so senior pupils at the school were transferred to Otterburn school. In 1975, the infants and juniors were moved to Otterburn and the Rector's School at Elsdon closed. The building is now used as an Inter-Church Field Centre in the care of a Warden who lives next door, in what was formerly the Head Teacher's house.

Byrness School opened in 1793 when Byrness Chapel was endowed. Louis Dutens' endowment made provision for a resident curate to teach, without charge, 12 children of poor parents living in the district. Vacancies were to be filled on the recommendation of the rector. Like other Church of England schools, Byrness is now integrated into the state system of education as a First School, but there are few children on the roll today.

Otterburn School, 1925

Otterburn School is now the main First School in the Upper Rede valley; it is not in the village, but almost a kilometre west, on the A696. The reason for this lies in the early history of the school. In the mid-19th century James Ferguson, a Scottish gardener, moved into what is now the Headmaster's house and began to give lessons in writing, arithmetic, the Bible and Catechism to some of the village children. Dunces were forced to translate 'aut disce aut discede' – either learn or get out! Thirty years later he too was forced to get out, when the Murrays bought the Otterburn estate, gave the school an endowment and appointed their own teacher. After 1870, the school was called Lady Murray's Church of England School. With the closure of Elsdon and Rochester Schools in this century, Otterburn School has expanded.

On the corner of the lane leading up to High Rochester stands a grey stone cottage. For over 100 years this functioned as Lord Redesdale's Church of England School, which he endowed in 1850 with an annual sum of £10 and a house and garden for the teacher. The original building consisted of the school house at the west end and a single large classroom with the scholars' porch at the east end. An extra classroom was provided after the turn of the century by converting the school house into the little classroom where girls were taught sewing; the teacher meanwhile was given a house in the village.

Winnie Foreman, who taught at Rochester school for 30 years, describes conditions there for scholars and staff, which were much the same as at other schools in Redesdale at that time.

Rochester School, Winnie Foreman fourth from right, at the back

In 1923 when she was 18, Winnie came from her home in North Seaton on the Northumberland coast, to Rochester, as a pupil teacher. She went home only during school holidays because of the difficulties involved in travelling. When the holiday was over, she had to have the Rector of Elsdon's permission to return on the first Monday morning of the new term, as there was no train on Sundays.

Most of her pupils were shepherds' children from outlying farms such as Rooken and Branshaw, now in ruins. 'They were better attenders than many of those who lived in the village', she says. Although there were plenty of books, other facilities were poor. There was no playground, so all P.E. lessons took place 'up the back road'. Since there was no school canteen, the pupils had to bring their own sandwiches for dinner; tea and cocoa were made by the teachers who boiled kettles on their classroom fire. Before dinner all the children had to wash their hands in water which the senior boys carried in buckets from the well at the roadside.

There was an occasional treat, such as the summer trip to the seaside at Whitley Bay. These excursions, started before 1923, are still a tradition for all primary school children in the valley.

Winnie reminisces about occasions such as that when Jock Scott and Hugh Tully absconded at dinner time to follow the Border Hunt as it passed. They reappeared just before the end of afternoon school, triumphantly brandishing the fox's bloody mask and brush. These trophies were hidden in the girls' porch while the boys faced the Headmaster's wrath. In 1953 the school was closed and its pupils transferred to Otterburn.

Farming

For almost 5,000 years, farming has been the principle occupation in Redesdale. This long tradition was established by the Neolithic people who were the first to settle permanently in the area. It is remarkable that apart from an increasing emphasis on stock and the improvement of land management, the basic pattern of hill farming has remained virtually unchanged in the Rede valley since these early times.

Early Farmers

Prehistoric farmers sited their settlements above the boggy valley floor, but below the ridge which would give them shelter from the prevailing wind and, most important, near fresh water. The same sites were favoured by later generations of Redesdale farmers, who unwittingly built their dwellings close to those of their prehistoric forbears – Girsonfield, Rattenraw and Netherhouses, for instance.

Rigg and furrow cultivation marks

The provision of yards in these early farms and the discovery by excavation of the bones of sheep, cattle and goats, confirm the practice of animal husbandry. The beasts bred then were much smaller than those of today, however. Prehistoric 'fields' associated with the settlements at Rattenraw and Yatesfield show lines of narrow rigg and furrow cultivation; elsewhere at Barracker Rigg and Blakeman's Law, the ground has been prepared for tilling – surface boulders have been deposited in 'cairns' around the edge of the cleared area or used to mark its boundaries.

Soil samples from the field have yielded pollen from cereals, beans and vetches, which suggests that the climate then was warm enough to grow these crops at higher altitudes than is now possible. Further evidence for arable farming comes from the considerable number of quern or grinding stones which have been found in prehistoric settlements, some discovered by excavation, but most turned up by the plough or picked up by people with an eye for an unusual worked stone. Quern-stones have been incorporated into local rockeries and garden walls; there is a good example at Otterburn Tower Hotel. More distinctive are the fluted querns in the porch of Horsley Church. Contemporary with those of the native British farmers, they show the influence of the Romans, garrisoned at High Rochester.

Fluted Roman Quern stone at Horsley Church and Quern stones used on Victorian garden pillar

The Roman troops demanded tribute from the local population – cereals, animal hides for uniforms, boots and tents. To meet this demand the farmers had to increase production, but when the Roman occupation ended towards the turn of the 5th century, the Britons probably returned to their old ways of subsistence farming. This way of life persisted for many centuries and was largely unaffected by the Anglian colonisation of the North. The Angles, whose more intensive methods of cultivation favoured the heavy clay soils of the coastal plain, were not interested in the poorer soils of the uplands.

Shieling

Farming communities in the Rede valley have always depended for their living on large grazing areas which extended to considerable distances from the home settlement; this land is still termed 'outbye'. The outbye often included land held in common and the open wastes beyond. Here all the flocks and herds were grazed together from April to August, while the 'inbye' land close to the settlement underwent cultivation. The animals which had survived winter on the harvest stubble and hungered in their byres, were driven out in the spring when the warmer weather encouraged the growth of new grass on the hillsides. These summer pastures were called summer steads or shieling grounds, and the temporary shelters built there by the herdsmen were known as shielings.

Queen Elizabeth I's historian William Camden who visited Redesdale in 1599, gave an eye-witness account of shieling:

> *Here every way round about in the wasts as they tearme*
> *them, you may see as it were the ancient Nomades, a*
> *martiall kinde of men, who from the moneth of Aprill unto*
> *August, lye out scattering and summering (as they tearme*
> *it) with their cattell in little cottages here and there which*
> *they call Sheales and Shealings.*

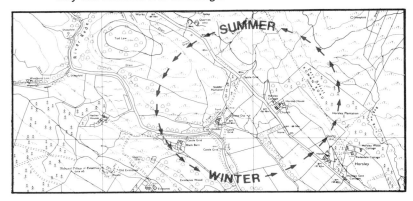

The main shieling grounds were listed in 1495 in the valuation of the estate of Sir Robert Tailbois, Lord of Redesdale. They included 7,000 hectares in Redesdale, at Spithope, Cottonshope, Birdhope, Chattlehope and Bateinghope, at Ridlees, Wilkwood, Thirlmoor and Sills. In many of these names the frequency of the suffix 'hope', which in local dialect means 'a sheltered valley for grazing', provides evidence for summering, in addition to the more obvious reference in names such as Davyshiels, Garretshiels and Whiskershiels.

James I's Border Survey of 1604 says that the 'Shielings Groundes' were used by 'the whole inhabitants of the Mannor, wherein each man knoweth his shieldinge steed; and they sheylde together by Surnames: not keepinge Cattle accordinge to the proporcion of the rent, but eatinge all in Common without stinte or number'.

Although the improved political situation on the Borders arising out of the succession of James VI and I in 1603 encouraged a return to more peaceful farming, the main obstacle to any real progress in Redesdale lay in the system of inheritance, traditional since before the Norman Conquest of 1066. When a man died his lands were divided equally amongst all his sons. As a result, by the late 17th century, not only were the land holdings too small to be farmed economically, but they also had to support a larger population. In addition, the continued sharing in common of the grazing grounds by both landowners and their tenants discouraged any basic improvements of upland pastures. What eventually stimulated radical changes in land management in the valley was the Enclosure Movement of the 18th and early 19th centuries.

Enclosures

Enclosure of common land, both arable and pasture, had been a continuing process in many parts of Northumberland since medieval times. In the troubled Border areas however, the system of customary tenure impeded enclosure. Here, landowners depended upon their tenants for military service and in return they offered low, fixed rents and the right to sub-let the tenancies. When peace was restored, tenants were no longer required to fight for their landlords. By the late 1600's the centuries-old practice of customary tenure was gradually replaced by leasehold, which gave landowners the opportunity to enclose moorland and hill pasture. Since this out-lying land was held in common, permission to enclose was usually obtained by an Act of Parliament, applied for by the landowner. The resulting Enclosure Award, together with a map, granted tenants parcels of land in return for the loss of their right of common pasture. The Award set out footpaths, bridleways, common quarries etc. One of the earliest Enclosure Awards in Redesdale was that for Elsdon Common in 1729.

*Quickthorn
(Hawthorn)*

Enclosure was to alter the landscape as dramatically as afforestation has done in the 20th century. It enabled landowners to create large fields of 8 to 40 hectares, bounded with earth banks planted with quickthorn to make a thick and impenetrable hedge. In the uplands the preferred method of enclosure was often dry-stone walls which, with sod-cast dykes, now snaked over the countryside. Stone stells and shooting butts dotted the hills and hopes as sheep and game became the main concerns of 19th century estate owners. Rough grazing was improved as farmers embarked on a programme of paring, burning, draining, manuring and liming the ground. Land which had been put down to oats and barley after 1603 frequently reverted to pasture. In these places today, the long shadows cast by the sun when low in the sky throw into high relief the broad bands of 17th century rigg and furrow cultivation.

Such changes in land utilisation were to have far-reaching effects in Redesdale. The decline in cereal production resulted in the closure of many flour mills. Of the 13 mills operating in the area in the mid-18th century, only those

*Remains of
corn drying kiln
at Tod Law*

51

at Elsdon and Grasslees still had a miller in residence when the National Census was taken in 1871. Grasslees ceased working soon after, but Elsdon continued milling into the 20th century, the last recorded date for a miller there being 1914. A more serious effect was the decline in the population. With fewer but larger agricultural units concentrating on sheep and game, there was less need for farm labourers, and once the rural industries had satisfied the landowners' demands for drainage tiles, lime etc., their workforces became redundant and joined the growing number of unemployed. Parish records show that many people became paupers, others sought work elsewhere and abandoned their farm steadings which soon fell into ruin. Some took the bigger step of leaving the country to build a new life in America. Not long after they were married at Elsdon, Adam Telfer and Jane Heslop sailed from Workington to New York. They eventually settled in Ontario, Canada, where their descendants still live. Jane's father, William Heslop, tenanted Cottonshopeburnfoot and wrote annually to his son-in-law. Some of William's letters for the period 1820–1840 have survived. They mention a large number of relatives and friends in Redesdale who had gone, or were about to go, to America and two who had decided to return. There is family news and much local gossip, ranging from the elopement of Peggy Wann 'who had been strictly guarded till the harvest' and the arrest of Simon Brown 'for robbing and attempting to murder a man in Newcastle' to changes in farm tenancies in the valley.

Like most farmers, William Heslop was concerned with the weather. In 1823 he wrote that there had been heavy snow in January:

> . . . some places on the road was past 12 feet deep all communication was stopped. Horses could not travel with the hay to the sheep – we had to carry it on our back for about a fortnight. Whiles carrying it, a whiles rolling it along and creeping hands and knees to keep us from sinking. The Tofthouse cows got no water for 9 days.

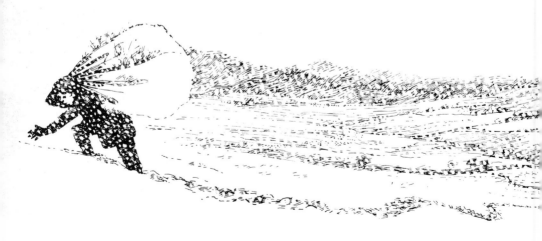

Fluctuations in the prices of bacon, beef, mutton, butter, tar, grease, flour and bread-meal were also discussed; the price of wool was of particular concern. In 1834, he nearly came to grief over his wool crop:

> *Wool was very high here last year 2 pound per stone and some more, but we did no good for Spithopehead Ramshope Chattlehope and us sold our wool unto a Galashiels man who broke. We still had our wool but it fell in price one fourth and is still so to this day. It is all sold now and gone at 30 shillings and some brass. So we lost one fourth or nearly so but still it is better than losing it all.*

Farming in the last hundred years

Until the Wool Marketing Board was set up in 1950, Redesdale farmers continued to sell the fleeces from their Cheviot and Blackface sheep privately or at auction marts. Shepherds got the clarts (dung-soiled fleece) or sometimes roadsters (gypsies) bought it for a shilling or two. The introduction of artificial fibres after World War II brought down the price of wool and now it only forms a small part of the farmer's income. The increasing use of farm machinery also began at this time, but until then farming methods and conditions had altered little since William Heslop first wrote to Adam and Jane in 1820. Lawrence Corbett of Dykehead has described farming as he knew it sixty years ago, and as many other farmers in Redesdale remember it.

Rev. Newlands with fellow workers

'In those days communications were poor so families had to be self sufficient. Although there were fewer cattle than there are now, there was always a cow to provide milk and butter, there were poultry for eggs and two 30 stone pigs for bacon, sausages, black puddings, hams and potted meat. Vegetables from the garden in summer made a welcome change from potatoes and turnips which we ate all winter. Flour and sugar were bought by the 10 stone bag from the grocer Tom Simpson who came with horse and cart from Wood-burn. It was also possible to buy groceries and other goods at the local shop, now the Snack Bar, in Rochester, which sold everything from dolls' eyes to corset laces! Bills were usually paid every six months when the shepherds got their wages.

Everything was home baked on the big black kitchen range, which was fired with peat or coals. When I was a callant I would take a horse and cart to the pits at Hareshaw or Elsdon and lead coals for the village folk. I got 7s 6d a load; the coal was 1s a cwt and there were 12 cwt in a cart-load.

When they left school the boys helped on the farm or were hired out and once the token sum of 2s 6d was paid to the herd lad, the hiring was considered binding for the next 6 months. The girls either went into service in a big house, were hired out to another shepherd's wife, or stopped at home and milked the cows, fed the calves, made butter, bread and candles and scrubbed everything!

Although the farms were isolated, families were never lonely. We looked forward to the postie who came on foot, every other day, or to the travelling tailor Jack Mowatt from Rothbury. He brought tweed patterns (samples) and stayed with us overnight, taking orders and measurements for suits and the like. There was Birdhopecraig Meeting House to attend on Sunday and visit-ing in the evenings. The clippie mats on the kitchen floor were rolled back as several families got together for a dance and supper.

It was still a hard life. In winter, loose hay – there weren't any bales then – had to be bundled in old sheets and carried on our backs, to the sheep. There was no sileage and turnips were grown only in the wartime and then just to feed

54

the cattle, not the sheep. The beasts were given natural linseed or cotton cake – with no added vitamins or minerals.'

Farms were poorer, the land was poorer, and it had to support more people. Apart from the large families, there were often 2 or 3 hired labourers, because boys of 14 could be hired for as little as £12–£14 for half a year. Wages were low and the herdsmen were frequently paid in kind. Potatoes, oatmeal and a fat sheep often supplemented their wages. The sheep would be shared with 2 or 3 neighbouring families because the meat would not keep. In the winter months the carcass was hung in the hayshed. The meat grew green with mould, but when cleaned and cooked it was delicious. Sometimes the shepherds got 'pack wages' i.e. several sheep for themselves. This had its disadvantage: if the price of sheep fell that year, then the shepherds' wages fell.

One aspect of farming which has not changed since Neolithic times is the reliance placed by man on his herd dog. In the past the dog's duty was to defend the flock from bears and wolves and to prevent the sheep from straying. The type of dog capable of performing these tasks was vastly different in size and temperament from today's working collie, whose function is the efficient control of the flock. A shepherd's work would be immeasurably more difficult without the assistance of his well-trained dog, for the collie's speed and agility far surpasses that of his master. The dog's worth is gauged by the facility with which he carries out his master's commands; this is tested daily on the farm, and at local, national and international sheep-dog trials; the first ever sheep-dog trial in England was held at Byrness in 1876.

Drovers and Smugglers

Major road developments occurred in Redesdale in the 18th and 19th centuries when the Turnpike Trusts improved communications by laying down new roads and resurfacing old ones. This was the first time such work had been carried out since the Romans built their road system through the valley to speed the passage of Imperial troops, messengers and traders. Dere Street followed a direct route to the north, taking no account of ancient trackways criss-crossing the fells and, like them, it recognised no political border, either tribal or national.

Many of the prehistoric ridge routes continued to be used in early medieval times, by Scottish drovers bringing sheep and cattle to the markets at Elsdon and Stagshaw Bank, near Corbridge. The reivers of the 16th century brought a temporary halt to this traffic and large-scale droving was not resumed until the 17th century. Village commons and Roman stations such as Chew Green and High Rochester provided a convenient resting place for the beasts on their ambling journey through Redesale, while their drovers took their ease in isolated roadside inns which have long since vanished. The village of Elsdon lay at the centre of this network of drove roads and feeder tracks. In 1762 the rector, the Rev Dodgson remarked on the number of Scottish carriers who frequented the local hostelries. The traffic was not all south-bound, for the Redesdale men took coal and lime by pack horse and later by cart north to the big estates in lowland Scotland. Besides the drovers and carriers there were others on the roads whose purpose was more furtive; they were the whisky smugglers.

In the late 18th century whisky was the favourite tipple of the working classes, but successive Governments believed that it was responsible for many crimes of violence. In an effort to reduce such crimes and to raise revenue, Parliament increased the excise duty on the sale of whisky, with the inevitable consequence that smuggling became a profitable, if somewhat risky, business conducted mainly from the Scottish side of the Border. Infamous characters such as 'Whisky' Jack Kane and Black Rory had illicit stills tucked away in the more remote Border valleys, one of them not far from Carter Bar itself! The enterprising Scots were only too willing to keep the inhabitants of Redewater supplied with whisky.

The dealers and their clients resorted to all manner of devious means to trick the two Excise Officers stationed at Rochester. One of these officers was William Coulson, who in the early 1850s excavated the Roman fort at High Rochester and the stone tombs at Petty Knowes; the smuggling fraternity must have been very satisfied by his interest in archaeology. They happily accepted regular orders for 'knives and forks', 'new milk' and 'grey hens' – the stoneware jars which contained the whisky. The jars, hidden in sacks of meal, were carried by pack horse to the lonely farms and inns. Carriers on legitimate business made ideal smugglers. One can imagine the satisfaction of the suspicious Excise Officer who commanded a carrier to open the empty coffin he was transporting and found it full of 'grey hens'!

Although the Officers had some successes (early 19th century records show an average of 50 prosecutions a year in Northumberland) there must have been many smugglers who evaded capture by employing skills and methods developed by their reiving ancestors. The Redesdale folk resented the Excise agents, more especially after 1820 when local men were no longer considered reliable for the position. Everyone from wealthy gentry to paupers connived to outwit them. Some of the gentry found their taste for whisky was stronger than their devotion to their magisterial duties, while old people and children allowed themselves to be used as smugglers because their poverty made it pointless to impose the heavy fines when they were caught.

Otterburn

The Emporium of Redesdale.

Hodgson, 1627

The derivation of the name 'Otterburn' is obvious, although it is many years since the last otter was seen in the burn. Of little significance whilst Elsdon was the capital of Redesdale, Otterburn came into its own with the building of the road, now the A696, into Scotland. Elsdon was bypassed and Otterburn, lying astride the new road, became a centre of trade for the area. In 1827 John Hodgson wrote, 'This place is the emporium of Redesdale. It is neat, and well built and has the appearance of industry, thrift and comfort about it.'

The village was already well-established when Gilbert de Umfraville, Lord of Redesdale 'died in Passion week' in 1245. A list of his property in Otterburn mentions 67 hectares of arable land and 17 hectares of meadow. There were cottages and land for 10 bondagers, freemen's cottages and 'a malting' i.e. a brew-house. By 1330 there was a water corn mill on the Otter Burn and a park 'containing nearly a league in circuit, in which are certain wild animals'. These elements conjure up a picture of a well-ordered rural community, indicative of peace and stability. All this was to change with the advent of the Anglo-Scottish wars by the end of the 14th century.

It is not known when or by whom Otterburn Tower was built, but it was certainly standing in 1388. Shortly before the Battle of Otterburn took place in August that year, the Scots, according to the Chronicler Sir John Froissart, laid siege to the Tower. They 'attacked it so long and unsuccessfully that they were fatigued, and therefore sounded a retreat'. In 1436 the Tower was owned by the Vice-Admiral of England, Sir Robert de Umfraville, last of the line. The Halls acquired the Tower in the early 16th century and it remained in their possession until 1745.

Otterburn Tower

'Mad' Jack Hall

The most notorious occupant of the Tower was Judge (or 'mad') Jack Hall, who was, though he later denied it, a willing participator in the Jacobite Rebellion of 1715. Like the Earl of Derwentwater, he was taken prisoner at the Battle of Preston and was tried for treason. He was found guilty and after five nerve-racking reprieves, he was eventually hanged, drawn and quartered at Tyburn.

In 1812 the novelist Sir Walter Scott, researching Border folklore, was a guest in the Tower.

Throughout the 19th century, a succession of owners continued to make alterations to the building. It was Thomas James of Beaufront near Hexham who incorporated what remained of the Tower into a lavish Victorian Gothic mansion, set in wooded grounds. It is now an hotel, and the rambling house still retains a little of the history of the old Tower. Concealed beneath a trapdoor in the floor is the deep well which once provided the inhabitants with their water supply.

Otterburn Hall lies about a kilometre north of the village, just off the road to the Army Training Camp. Its grandiose appearance belies its true age. The architectural design is Elizabethan, but it was built as recently as 1870 for Lord James Murray, youngest son of the Duke of Atholl. The pseudo-Elizabethan bricks were manufactured from clay quarried on the site. During the Second World War the Hall was used as a military hospital and many of the location shots for the wartime film *Dangerous Moonlight* starring Anton Walbrook and Sally Grey, were shot there. Today, Otterburn Hall is a popular holiday and conference centre and the old clay quarry an attractive boating lake.

Otterburn Hall

The origins of The Percy Arms in the centre of Otterburn lie in the 18th century when cattle drovers using the riverside track through the valley stopped for liquid refreshment at the tiny inn by the bridge over the Otter Burn. The inn was named in honour of the Duke of Northumberland who became Lord of the Manor of Otterburn in 1769. About this time four adjacent terraced cottages to the west of the inn were taken over to accommodate the increasing number of travellers who were using the new Turnpike road in Redesdale. The Redesdale Arms, or 'The First and Last', further north, probably owes its existence to this road.

In the early 19th century The Percy Arms became an important staging post for the London to Edinburgh passenger-mail coaches 'Chevy Chase' and 'Blucher', which plied the Newcastle–Jedburgh run. The guards and drivers, who wore red coats and white hats, blew the long brass post-horn as their coach passed the little school – much to the delight of the pupils. The development of the railways, with stations at Kirkwhelpington and Woodburn, brought coaching to an end and the inn began to decline. Like the school, it was taken over in 1870 by the Murrays when they bought the Otterburn Estate, and the inn was renamed The Murray Arms. The Estate ws sold by auction in 1920, and the sign has now reverted to The Percy Arms.

The inn's former clientèle included Harry the Skinner, who with his donkey, frequented the farms, buying up sheepskins; Thomas Gillespie, cleaner of clocks and watches and self-appointed village doctor; the infamous Sally the Mugger 'a mighty woman of Herculean build', who hawked cartloads of poached salmon round the district every autumn.

Otterburn Mill lies on the southern outskirts of the village, probably starting out as the corn mill mentioned in Gilbert de Umfraville's will of 1245. When the mill was first used for 'fulling' (cleaning and thickening cloth) is not certain, but as late as 1914, long after the mill was a working woollen mill, farmers were still bringing grain to be crushed.

From 1728, for nearly 60 years, the Beighatt family owned the mill and produced woollen cloth. But it was in the 19th century that the Waddells made Otterburn Mill world-famous for its tweeds and blankets. In 1821 William Waddell came from Jedburgh with his family of 12 children, to settle in Otterburn, taking over the old fulling mill there. At that time the cloth trade in rural

Northumberland was still a cottage-based industry. Whilst clothiers bought the shorn fleeces, farming families found that they could supplement their income in the winter months by combing, carding and spinning the wool before it was put out to the weavers. Such was the Waddells' reputation for carding however, that farmers' wives had them process the wool before they did the spinning. When the weavers had completed their task, the cloth was sent back to the Waddells for final treatment before sale.

Eventually the clothiers found it more convenient to concentrate the different skills of their industry under one roof, in urban areas where labour was plentiful. As a result of this trend, the Waddells decided to install their own hand-looms in the mill.

Having now set up as weavers, the family began to specialise in making tweeds, blankets and rugs. Their woollen cloth was so hard-wearing that it was known locally as 'bull's lug' – a term still used in Northumberland for any coarse, heavy cloth. Otterburn Mill continued to produce cloth until 1977 when competition from man-made fibres forced closure. The old mill is now used as a warehouse, shop and showroom; the tweeds are made in the Waddells' other mill at Wetheral near Carlisle and the woollen goods on sale at the Otterburn Mill are the products of other specialist manufacturers. In addition to the traditional fabrics and knitwear, leather, jewellery and ceramics have broadened the scope of the enterprise, which remains in the ownership of William Waddell's descendants.

There was a time, however, when rugs and blankets were often called 'Otterburns'. Such was their renown that Queen Victoria when requiring a travelling rug was known to ask for her 'Otterburn'.

...ully care, actually improves with washing. lasts for years and, if washed with Every hour of the twenty-four, waking or sleeping, your Baby could not have a more faithful guardian against Baby chills and ills than this honest Otterburn Rug. For Cot or Cradle it makes a cosy Blanket; when Baby "walks out" it does protecting duty as a pram rug; indoors, it makes the snuggest Nursing Wrap.

Handy, yet ample in size, the "Otterburn" measures 36 ins. by 30 ins. and is made in 14 Self-shades and in 6 Two-tones. The Self-shades are known as the Standard Range and the Two-tones are attractively designed in pastel toned overchecks. Ask to see colour ranges.

The "Big Otterburn" is more than an ideal Crib Rug. Though originally intended as a protector of Baby's sleeptime, its size—54 ins. by 36 ins.—has earned it favour as a general purpose Rug for individual use in a hundred ways. The colour range is exactly the same as for the 36 ins. by 30 ins. size (above).

The Otterburn Toy Pram Rug is, as its name suggests, a miniature of the well-known Otterburn Baby Rug. It measures 20 ins. by 15 ins., and helps earnest "Little Mothers" to walk out Dolly looking just like Baby's—and i... shades of the stand...

Rural Industries

For the cole mynes; ther is not anie in use at this tyme, the inhabitants having suche store of turf and peate as they will not bestowe their labor in getting of coles, but if the Cuntrie weare inhabited by industrious people and men of trade, the mynes would bee of great value.

Survey of the Debateable and Border Land, 1604

Agricultural advances in the 19th century stimulated the growth of rural industries and Redesdale quickly followed the general trend. Farmers needed lime and drainage tiles and since Redesdale was fairly inaccessible local resources had to provide the raw materials.

Coal

By the end of the 18th century most of the old forest of Redesdale had disappeared and, although some people burnt peat, coal was now the main domestic fuel. Coal was also needed to fire lime, brick and tile kilns and to smelt iron at Ridsdale and at Hareshaw, near Bellingham. Since transport costs from the Tyneside collieries were prohibitive, there was every inducement to tap local coal resources. Outcrops of poor quality coal in the district were found to be readily accessible and easily worked.

Indeed coal had already been worked for some time in Redesdale. The burial on 17 July 1691 of a relative of William Ward 'colyer at Rattenraw' is recorded in the Elsdon Parish Register. By 1750 there were 'collieries' at Yatesfield, Elsdon, Carrick, Raw, High Shaw and Blackblakehope. At the end of the century Grasslees, Pengeford, Bellsheil, Bush, Wilkwood, Rooken, Brownrigg and Swindon were also working. Other pits were opened later, but few were in production for long. Most of the 'collieries' were short adit mines or groups of bell pits. The bell pit was a single shallow shaft sunk to the depth at which a workable seam was reached. The miners worked outwards, extracting the coal to the radius which experience had shown to be the limit of safety. Having exhausted the possibilities of one shaft, further coal was won by digging a succession of pits following the seam. To reduce the danger of roof collapse, the rule of thumb method was to separate shafts by the distance a miner could throw his shovel when he stood on top of the slag heap beside the shaft. The seams varied in thickness from roughly a metre near Dunshiel to less than 22cm near Silloans. Much of the coal was splint coal, that is mixed with bands of shale and only suitable for firing kilns; however larger workings at Brownrigg and Elsdon yielded better quality coal for domestic use.

A number of landowners engaged the services of two of the most competent

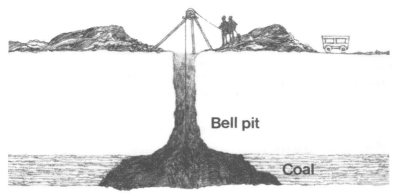

Bell pit

Coal

and respected colliery surveyors of the early 19th century, John Buddle and John Watson, who advised on the feasibility of opening up coal workings in Redesdale. Their reports were not very encouraging. In 1806, Watson estimated that the outlay for establishing a colliery at Birdhopecraig would be as much as £556 10s 0d. On top of that there were the running costs – pumping out water, wages for those extracting coal and maintaining the equipment, candles, coal tubs, pit props, keeping the horse etc. For example to run Rooken Pit for 10 months in 1827/8 cost £177 14s 6d; the coal sold in that period only fetched £145 12s 0d. Mining was obviously not a highly profitable business here so there was little incentive to invest in complicated and expensive machinery. Further difficulties were that many of the seams were heavily faulted and even in the shallower workings flooding was a major problem.

The number of men actually engaged in mining in Redesdale was always small. In the 1841 Census, 22 out of a total male population of 852 were listed as miners and in 1871, 28 out of 758. Mining was very much a 'family' business. Five members of the Turnbull family worked Brownrigg, Highshaw and Rooken between 1792 and 1841; thirteen members of the Proudlock family worked at Swindon, Low Carrick and Ovenstone between 1808 and 1871. In the 1871 Census Michael Hamilton, his three sons and his 15 year old daughter Janet are listed as miners at Monkridge Hall. The miners did not own their pits but leased them from the landowners. The owners erected cottages, for example at Brownrigg, Raylees, Monkridge and Swindon, and the leases often included small plots of land for gardens and pasture. There is little information about miners' wages at this time, but the overman at Garretshiels received 1s a week in 1803.

By 1910 all the smaller workings had ceased to operate, only Bellshiel and Elsdon remaining in production to supply local demands for domestic fuel. Bellshiel closed in 1935 and Elsdon in 1972. The only traces now of the mining industry in Redesdale are the grass-covered waste tips, silted-up bell pits, and the merchant's yard at Elsdon.

Lime

From the early 17th century lime was increasingly used on the land, but it was only in 1750 that the practice was introduced into north Northumberland. Records show that lime was burnt locally in Redesdale from about 1785–1887, with the greatest activity taking place between 1810–1830.

The majority of the kilns produced lime for use on the estate where they were built, any surplus being sold to neighbouring farmers. The exceptions were the kilns at Whitelee, Rooken and Greenchesters, which operated to supply the Scottish market. The biggest venture was at Greenchesters, where two kilns were working before 1803. The coal to fire these kilns was brought from Brownrigg colliery which was leased from 1806–1818 by John Davidson, the proprietor of the Greenchesters kilns. The Rooken kilns and the Whitelee Lime Works at the head of the Bateinghope Burn each worked two kilns using coal from nearby collieries. By the 1840s neither the coal nor the limestone reserves were capable of further economic exploitation, so Whitelee and Rooken had to be closed down. Only Greenchesters remained viable and continued to produce small quantities of lime until the 1880s, when it too ceased operation.

Limeworks were costly, not only to build but to work; fuel, transport and wages virtually cancelled out the profit. The poor quality of the local coal was partly responsible. Many late 18th century farming tenancies contained a lime clause to ensure that the tenant limed his land as required. The price of lime must therefore have been a source of anxiety for many farmers and to keep costs down, estate kilns were often operated by the tenant farmers and their labourers as a seasonal occupation.

The lime kilns have now collapsed to varying degrees and in some cases the bowls and eyes have been used as convenient tips for farm and domestic refuse. Usually enough survives to give an idea of how they must have looked and how they worked. The best and most accessible remains are those at Grasslees and Dykehead, but it is well worth the walk to see those at Whitelee, if only for the view down the valley.

Dykehead Limekiln, High Rochester

Coal and limestone were burned together to produce lime

Bricks and Tiles

Field drainage, particularly on the heavier upland soils, has always been a problem and where drainage was attempted it was either by shallow surface trenches or the traditional method of rigg and furrow. Tile drains first appeared in the North in the 1820s. These were a series of pipes made by standing an inverted U-sectioned tile on a flat tile or sole. The pipes were laid in the bottom of trenches which were then back-filled. In the late 1830s the introduction of machines to make cylindrical pipes provided a cheaper and more effective method of drainage. The Drainage Act of 1846 also gave impetus to land improvement by providing money at low interest rates to landowners and commercial companies.

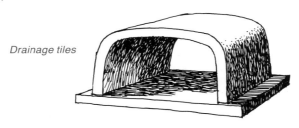

Drainage tiles

In Upper Redesdale three brick and tile kilns operated at Garretshiels, Ovenstone and Knightside. All the Redesdale kilns were sited near clay and coal deposits and produced drainage tiles of 5–15cm in diameter; they also made common bricks for lining the shafts in the local coal pits. The working life of the kilns was short, about twenty years. Garretshiels and Ovenstone started in the 1850s, had ceased production by the mid 1870s and Knightside, which was then just opening, was disused before 1887. Only at Garretshiels is there any evidence today of this past industry: the old kilns are now a piggery.

As with lime burning, the manufacture of bricks and tiles was a seasonal occupation, but those who fired the kilns were skilled workmen. Consequently they chose to seek employment elsewhere when the Redesdale kilns closed down.

Stone

Travellers using the A696 cannot fail to notice the huge spoil heaps stretching along the crest of Hunterlee Hill. This is the waste from Blaxter's Stone Quarry, first worked at the beginning of the 19th century. The grey sandstone was so easy to quarry and cut that output was fast and cheap and, as a result, demand was high. The first local dwelling reputedly built with stone from Blaxter's was the farmhouse at Raylees, in 1821. The stone was destined to travel much further – to Glasgow, St Andrew's, Omagh in Ireland, St Mary's College, Durham, much of Princes Street, Edinburgh and the Abbey at Iona, where it was used in restoration work. In 1984 the quarry reached the end of its profitable working life and was closed by its last owners, Tarmac.

Modern Developments

Catcleugh, Whitelee and the Halls

Whitelee and Catcleugh lie at the head of Redesdale. In this part of the valley the growing season is short, the snow lingers in the peat hags and the dead grass looks white on the fells in winter – hence the name, Whitelee. Long before Catcleugh reservoir was created, wild cats roamed the open woodland and rocky cleughs in the side valleys, and the name 'Cat Cloughe' was already well established when James I commissioned the *Border Survey* of 1604. For many centuries there were no permanent settlements at either place, but in the summer months farmers from lower down the valley would drive up their beasts and flocks to graze on the hill slopes. Whitelee and Catcleugh occur in the list of 'some pastures' in the 1604 survey. Catcleugh was shared by the Halls, Reeds and Hedleys who between them paid an annual rent of 3s 4d to the Crown; Whitelee, held by the Reeds, was valued at only 1s.

The present farm of Whitelee is the last settlement in England on the A68 through Redesdale. A herdsman's house was there by the late 17th century, when the property was owned by the Earl of Derwentwater. A coaching inn was built about 1767 to provide accommodation for travellers on the turnpike road. Inscribed on the lintel of the door were the words *'PAX SIT HUIC DOMO INTRANTIBUS'* (Peace to all who enter here). When the Newcastle and Gateshead Water Company bought the land for a reservoir, the inn was closed on the grounds that effluent from the building would contaminate the water.

Catcleugh Reservoir

Gabriel Hall who became High Sheriff of Northumberland in 1706, was one of the wealthiest landowners in Redesdale. Second son of Martin Hall of The Bog (renamed Brownchesters), near Otterburn, Gabriel bought Catcleugh and 400 hectares of summer pasture at Spithope for £440 in 1678. He went on to acquire a large number of landholdings in the valley, including 'Mad Jack' Hall's estate at Otterburn. Some of the boundary stones which marked the limits of Gabriel's land in Upper Redesdale, cut with his initials *G.H.,* can be seen near the Pennine Way as it runs across Brownrigg Head and Black Hill. Gabriel died at Otterburn Tower in 1727 aged 90, and was buried at Elsdon. Several of his estates at the head of the valley, amongst them Catcleugh, were bought in 1769 by the Duke of Northumberland. In 1889 the land was sold to the Newcastle and Gateshead Water Company and Gabriel's fine house, sheltered by woodland, now stands in solitude on the banks of the reservoir.

Catcleugh Reservoir, completed in 1905, was built to supply the growing population of Tyneside, from where most of the labour force was recruited. Between 800 and 1,000 men and their families had to be housed, fed and kept in order. Since the majority came from the rival towns of Newcastle and Gateshead, to prevent any outbreak of violence two 'villages', 'Newcastle' and 'Gateshead' were established on the site but on opposite sides of the Rede. 'Home' was a tin-roofed shack, 'Church' a wooden hut and schooling was provided for the children at Byrness. The job of teacher at this school must have been rather difficult for none of them ever stayed long. Supplies for the workers and their families were brought by rail to West Woodburn and then taken on a specially laid track to the site.

The temporary village

Unlike the recently completed Kielder reservoir, constructed with all the advantages of modern technology, Catcleugh was gouged out of the hillside by picks, shovels and muscle power. A huge steam navvy was brought in to speed up the work, but horse-drawn carts had to be used to carry away the earth, boulders and tree roots. Many of the labourers were suspicious of the new-fangled mechanisation, and preferred to use their hand tools which they had tried and found faithful. Those who could use a shovel left-handed to fill the carts were paid half a penny an hour more than the right-handed workers. The navvies earned £4 a week for a 12 hour day, and by all accounts this was the best paid job in Britain at that time. But many squandered their wages on drink and gambling, especially pitch and toss which was illegal and, not surprisingly, the local constabulary were kept busy.

Catcleugh can hold up to 2·305 million gallons, and its water is piped daily to the intermediate reservoirs at Colt Crag and Whittle Dene which supply Tyneside. During the first World War it was discovered that the water pressure to these reservoirs had decreased considerably; investigations showed that this was due to an accretion of sediment. The method of cleaning the pipe was to turn off the water supply for two weeks, when half the total length of the pipe was cleaned. After the water had been drained out, a gang of 6 to 8 men known as scrapers, wearing waterproof clothing, climbed down into the 75cm diameter pipe. Candles provided the light but they frequently went out and it was difficult to keep matches dry enough to relight them. Each man would lie on his back on a bogey or trolley, to scrape the walls of the pipe with a short-handled hoe. Two youths called putters, also on trolleys, followed the scrapers, shovelling the dirt into buckets from the bottom of the pipe where it had fallen. When the buckets were full, they were pulled out by ropes lowered by a workman standing over the nearest manhole. The men, who were local volunteers, were each paid 1s for every 3 metre section cleaned. Shifts were short, usually 6 hours, although the work was often completed in less time as the pipe was not a place in which to linger. The rest of the pipe was cleaned the following year.

The present method of cleaning is much easier and was introduced in 1943. After the water is shut off, a 1m section of pipe is removed and a tightly-fitting cylindrical brush is inserted. The section is replaced and the water is turned on again. The pressure forces the brush down the pipe to the Wood Ford near Swinburne, 35 km away. As the brush progresses the dirt which it has loosened is flushed out through sludge holes sited at every slack along the route.

The whole cleaning process which is carried out once a year by 20 instead of 120 men, takes only two days. It has none of the claustrophobic fascination of the earlier method, which fortunately is now as much part of history as are the Border Reivers.

Forestry and Byrness

Forestry in this century has provided some of the employment previously created by more traditional industries. The Forestry Commission was established in 1919 and 11 years later it purchased a plot of land in Upper Redesdale from the Duke of Northumberland. This was the beginning of the modern Redesdale Forest. Further landholdings were gradually acquired, so that Redesdale is now part of a much larger complex of tree planting known collectively as Kielder Forest – 50,000 hectares of moorland planted with over a million trees. A cold climate, an exposed position and wet, infertile soil have dictated the species of trees which can be grown, mainly Sitka spruce, Norway spruce, Scots pine, lodgepole pine and Japanese larch.

During the depression of the 1930s, the forest provided much needed work for many people. Labourers built roads and bridges and ploughed up the land prior to tree planting. During the Second World War, German and Italian prisoners-of-war who made the road from the A68 to Cottonshope wrote their names for posterity in the concrete used in the construction of various culverts. After the war, refugees from Latvia and Estonia were given employment planting trees.

At first the labour force was housed in a temporary camp, then in 1936–7 the Forestry Commission built two houses at the Raw, two at Byrness and two at Cottonshopeburnfoot. While the forest was being established there was plenty of work and it became necessary to build a complete village to house the foresters and their families. The site chosen was at Byrness. The scheme provided for 47 houses, shops, a school, a church and a village hall. Though the cycle of thinning, felling and replanting continues in the Redesdale Forest, much of the work which formerly was done by a large work force is now mechanised. This, together with increased productivity, has meant that despite a rise in the production of timber the requirement for forest workers is far less now than was envisaged at the time the village was built. Few of the

Byrness

houses in Byrness are now occupied by Forestry Commission employees. Of those surplus to Commission requirements, some are let to workers in other local industries while the remainder standing empty are to be sold.

For a number of years now the Forestry Commission has been aware of the attraction which their quiet plantations hold for city dwellers. In an attempt to make these more accessible the 20km Forest Drive from Blakehopeburn-haugh to Kielder was opened in 1973: but be warned, the road isn't tarmac all the way. There are parking spaces, picnic areas, splendid viewpoints and a variety of walks and nature trails for the visitor, who may like to combine the drive through the forest with an outing to Kielder Reservoir. Additional picnic sites, for the use of those travelling on the A68 through Redesdale, lie just off the main road at Blakehopeburnhaugh, Cottonshopeburn and Byrness.

The Otterburn Training Area

In 1910, Europe was drifting unavoidably towards war. Winston Churchill, Home Secretary in the last Liberal Government, was staying with Lord Redes-dale and happened to comment that the broad expanse of empty moorland in the area would make an excellent artillery range. From that chance remark stemmed the whole concept of the Redesdale All Arms Training Area. It became a reality in 1911, when the War Office bought its first property in the district, the Featherwood Estate. The rest of the Sills Burn valley, owned mainly by Lord Redesdale was purchased in March the following year.

Initially the range was to be used by the Royal Artillery, so accommodation was necessary for both men and horses. Troops and their officers were billeted in tents on Birdhopecraig, but once the camp became permanent, the first buildings to be erected were stables for the horses. A wooden hut served as a military hospital. All the catering was done by cooks from the units who were using the Training Area; the troopers mess was a large marquee. Bird-hopecraig Hall, Lord Redesdale's old shooting box, was the officers mess; it was destroyed by fire in the 1960's. Until 1947 all supplies were brought by rail to Woodburn Station, from where they were carried by cart and later by lorries, up to the Camp. After 1947, everything was conveyed by motorised transport.

67th Batt. Royal Field Artillery, arriving at Woodburn Station

Throughout the training period the men worked hard. It was a six-day week and even Sunday's Church parade in the Camp on the seventh day, was compulsory. The days were long. The men were up at 6 a.m. to feed and water their horses. After breakfast it was out on the range for target practise at Featherwood. When they returned to camp in the evening their first concern had to be their horses, which not infrequently were wet and muddy. There was little opportunity for relaxation – no T.V., cinema or trips into town to see the bright lights. Instead they could spend what remained of the evening in the Reading Tent, where there were newspapers, books and facilities for writing letters.

From 1911 to 1954 the War Office, now the Ministry of Defence gradually acquired more property in Upper Redesdale and Upper Coquetdale and a second Camp, now the main Camp, was built at Otterburn. The Otterburn Training Area as it is known today, is the largest military training ground in the British Isles. It covers 56,000 acres, much of it in the Northumberland National Park. There are 30 tenanted farms on the Estate and the Camps provide much-valued employment for 100 local civilians. Otterburn is used throughout the year by all branches of the armed services; the men still train hard, but they also have time to enjoy themselves.

Redesdale Experimental Husbandry Farm

Farming has always been the most important industry in Redesdale and it is appropriate that one of the Country's twelve Experimental Farms has been set up in the valley. Redesdale Experimental Husbandry Farm is situated on the south side of the A68, near Horsley. It was established in 1967 by the Ministry of Agriculture, Fisheries and Food, to provide information and advice for the farming industry. Each of these centres is representative of a different type of farming in England and Wales; Redesdale specialises in problems associated with hill land.

The farm comprises three holdings – Ashtrees, Cleughbrae and Dargues, giving a total area of 1,569 hectares. Most of the land is hill pasture and apart from a few shelter belts of conifers, is fairly exposed. The experimental work carried out by the full-time staff is mainly concerned with improving poor quality pasture and the successful rearing and fattening of lambs for the consumer market.

Upgrading of rough pasture has been achieved by applying herbicide to kill the native vegetation first, then growing turnips as a forage crop and re-seeding with grass and clover. Other methods of land improvement are currently being evaluated. Local farmers have been quick to follow the methods advocated by the Experimental Husbandry Farm and, as a result, some striking changes in the landscape of the Rede valley have taken place during the last ten years. In winter, the fresh green of the reclaimed land stands out in marked contrast to the withered brown of the surrounding hillsides.

Advances in animal husbandry have also been made. The Redesdale farm runs approximately 140 cows, but its main work is with sheep, in particular the blackface breed which is best suited for this type of hill land. Successful experiments have been carried out into the nutritional needs of ewes at tupping time and in the winter months, also into the control of unattractively named diseases such as head-fly and scrapie. Early recognition and treatment of these disorders is essential if unnecessary wastage is to be avoided. Another important technique developed at Redesdale EHF has been the early weaning of one twin lamb onto grass leaving the other with its mother.

Farmers are encouraged to visit the centre, by appointment, to see the work in progress and the new methods employed. In an effort to make the general public more aware and consequently more appreciative of the value of its function, the farm holds an annual open day during the first week in August.

Endpiece

Life in Redesdale has changed little over the centuries. It started as a farming community and still is a farming community. It became a forward base camp and training area during the Roman occupation and today houses the largest training area for NATO forces in Europe. The people are the same close knit community they have always been although nowadays more sober, honest and thrifty. They have had a hard life through the ages and, as often happens in such communities of people who are close knit by ties of kinship, comradeship or feud, their friends or foes are characterised by pet names almost as tokens of affection.

Whitetoppen of the Raw	Capability
Ill drowned George	Noddy
Nebless Clem	Digger
Jocke with the lippe	Shack
Pikehood	The Doc
Jessy the Babb	Baldy
Hoggskins Hedley	The Vicar
Trailer	Jack the Rabbit or the Battling Bunny
Halting Will	Pastor
Gleed Hob or Hob the Tailor	Tosh
Black Jokk	Dinger

These names may be an enigma to outsiders but an exact description, to those who know, of a physical or character trait or of some accident that has occurred. Of the two lists one is from the 16th and 17th centuries, the other from the present day. We leave it to you to decide what the names signify.

Glossary

Affray	fighting in a public place
Ballista	catapult
Barmkin	a walled enclosure
Bondager	tenants who owed labour service
Bothy	turf hut
Caistrel	kestrel
Callant	lad or stripling
Chattels	possessions
Cist	grave
Dene	open valley
Evil Eye	witchcraft
Felons	criminals
Haugh	low-lying land by a river
Hot-trod	immediate pursuit
Kirk	church
Kye	cows
Monolith	single standing stone
Pilasters	shallow piers attached to a wall
Pinfold	a pound for stray livestock
Reiving	stealing, taking by force
Slack	a dip in the land
Spate	flood
Stell	a gathering place for sheep, a fold
Stob	head
Taties	potatoes
Tithes	parishioners annual tax of one tenth, usually payable in kind to support the clergy and church
Toon	town
Watches	lookouts
Wintersteeds	winter grazing grounds, usually the stubble of cultivated fields nearest the village

Acknowledgements

The author is grateful to the Northumberland County Record Office for permission to consult the Delaval papers and the W.P. Hedley Manuscripts, to Margaret Mitcheson, Peggy Telfer and Francis Corbett for their help and to the many people of Redesdale who were willing to talk about their valley.